The Lowfat Mexican Cookbook

True Mexican Taste Without The Waist

by Robert H. Leos
and Nancy A. Leos

R & E Publishers
Saratoga, California

The Lowfat Mexican Cookbook
True Mexican Taste Without the Waist

Published by
R&E Publishers
P.O. Box 2008
Saratoga, CA 95070
Phone: (408) 866-6303
Fax: (408) 866-0825

Typesetting by Diane Parker
Cover Design by Kaye Quinn

ISBN 0-88247-896-6
Library of Congress 91-050690

PRINTED IN THE UNITED STATES OF AMERICA

Contents

PREFACE

HORS D'OEUVRES AND ACCOMPANIMENTS

SOUPS AND SALADS

AN ENCHILADA VARIETY

SEAFOOD SPECIALTIES

MEAT AND POULTRY

Preface

Mexican food is now an American favorite. You hardly have to venture far these days to sample this tasty cuisine with "south of the border" roots. Check the lunch crowds at Mexican restaurants all across the United States. Witness the growing number of restaurants featuring familiar tacos and enchiladas with sauce ranging from a mild tomato sauce to the scorching heart pounders like chipotle and New Mexico pepper sauce. Classic dishes from southern Mexico are gaining in popularity in the United States as are "Tex-Mex" dishes known for the not-so-mild flavor of serrano, jalapeño, and piquín peppers. Some of the country's finest hotels now feature a Mexican brunch complete with migas, huevos rancheros, fajitas, and pico de gallo—all adorned with molcajetes, strolling guitarristas, and art from the southwest United States. Fajitas and breakfast tacos are hot items from south Texas to New York City, from the west coast to the east, and into our nation's capital. And while baseball fans are enjoying one of the nation's favorite sports, more nachos are consumed than the classic American hot dog.

Even as the popularity of Mexican food continues to grow, many consumers are becoming aware of the fact that Mexican food can be very fattening in its traditional preparation. *The Lowfat Mexican Cookbook* is written to minimize the use of additional and unnecessary oils and still maintain loyalty to Mexican and spicy regional Tex-Mex flavors.

Here are a few observations that form the basis of *The Lowfat Mexican Cookbook* and the recipes in it.

In many Mexican restaurants we always look forward to those baskets of tortilla chips that are brought to the table with the drinks and hot sauce. Many restaurants serve generous amounts of chips, hot sauce, cheese, and guacamole *before* the main course. Then comes hot "refried" beans, more guacamole, rice, chile con queso, the main dish, wheat flour tortillas, flan, and sopapillas. Most of these contain large amounts of fat as prepared traditionally and contribute, at least in our case, to an inevitable weight gain, at the least, and possible health problems, at the worst.

To further place this into context, let's use the tortilla chips as an example. The Surgeon General of the United States suggests a diet in which less than thirty percent of calories consumed are made up of fat. At nine calories per gram of fat, this means that a diet of 1500 calories per day should have no more than 50 grams of fat (30% of 1500 = 450 calories ÷ 9 calories per gram of fat = 50 grams per day). Some commercially prepared fried tortilla chips contain about seven grams of fat for sixteen fried chips. This translates to perhaps as much as fourteen to twenty grams of fat in just one basket of chips. This is more than a fourth of the recommended fat for an entire day! And we haven't even ordered the main course! On the other hand, corn tortillas, about four inches in diameter, simply heated, not fried, have about one gram of fat, or about as much as in a slice of whole wheat bread. The same tortilla, baked, serves as several crispy chips, a chalupa shell, or nachos, all without the additional oil from frying. The point here is that the excessive use of oils in frying tortilla chips and cooking beans, rice, and many of the other foods served substantially increases the amount of fat consumed (and therefore the calories). Certainly we hear about oils that manufacturers are calling "good" oils (those with more polyunsaturates), but "good" oils are still 100% fat. Look at the labels of your favorite "good" oils such as safflower and canola oil and you will see that fat makes up 100% of all the calories in a single tablespoon of oil. So fat is fat, no matter in what form.

Another major contributor to the fat content in Mexican food cooking is cheese. Ounce for ounce, cheese contains at least as much saturated fat as a lean piece of beef. Cheese is almost all saturated fat and, for that reason, it is used sparingly in these recipes. As with any recipe, the amount of cheese, pepper, salt, and other ingredients should be adjusted to suit your tastes. Reduced-fat cheeses are available in a variety of flavors, and unless otherwise noted, the cheddar used in these recipes is the reduced-fat variety with five grams of fat per ounce instead of the usual eight or more.

What about meat and poultry? Recipes in *The Lowfat Mexican Cookbook*, with the exception of fajitas, call for top round steak, skinless chicken, and lean pork. We realize that these meats contain higher amounts of fat than grains, vegetables, and legumes, all of which are part of Mexican cooking and part of this book. The intent of *The Lowfat Mexican Cookbook*, however, is not to discourage the use of meat but to encourage careful selection and preparation. For additional information, the fat, calorie, cholesterol, protein, and carbohydrate content of each of the recipes is included in the Nutritional Index of this book.

Using the Microwave Oven With These Recipes

Some of the recipes are written with directions for the microwave oven. Although most recipes simply call for heating of enchiladas, nachos, and other foods, precautions should be always be taken to ensure your safety and maintain the quality of your food. For example, you will see "Cover" used in some recipes. Whether you use a glass cover or plastic, precautions should be taken to avoid being burned by steam escaping when the cover is removed after cooking. If you use plastic wrap as a cover, this can be avoided by leaving a small corner of the covering open during cooking to allow steam to escape.

All dishes should be specifically microwave oven safe and directions for heating and cooking in your microwave oven should be used and followed closely.

All the recipes that include directions for the microwave oven have been tested on a 700-watt, variable control (ten power levels) oven. For the purpose of simplicity, HIGH (100%), MEDIUM (50%), and LOW (10%) are used in all the recipes.

There are now many microwave cookbooks on the market. Most agree that the best way to use a microwave oven is to cook using the minimum time, test for doneness, and cook longer if necessary. This general rule will virtually eliminate the common problem of overcooking.

Using either conventional or microwave oven cooking methods, we hope you will agree that *The Lowfat Mexican Cookbook* serves as a useful reminder that delicious Mexican food does not have to be fattening. On the contrary, you may be surprised that there is no loss of the fantastic flavors and spices that make this cuisine one of the world's most popular.

Very happy lowfat cooking!

Robert H. Leos and Nancy A. Leos
Austin, Texas
1992

Hors D'oeuvres and Accompaniments

Lowfat tortilla chips for dipping and for nachos.

Peppers and Hot Sauces. A brief description of some peppers commonly used in Mexican cooking.

Salsa Picosa de Tomate. Peppers, onion, jalapeños or serranos, and numerous spices, are blended into a spicy table sauce.

Salsa de Tomatillo. Tomatillos are small, green tomatoes, used to make a sauce quite different from the red tomato-based sauce described previously.

New Mexico Red Pepper Sauce. Made with large dried New Mexico peppers, garlic, salt, and onion.

Pico de Gallo. Chopped peppers, onion, tomatoes, cilantro, black pepper, water, lime juice, and white wine vinegar.

Chipotle Sauce. The smoke-flavored spicy sauce made from the chipotle pepper.

Basic Nachos. A crisp corn tortilla chip snack with cheese, onion, peppers, and sometimes beans, beef, or chicken.

Frijoles Refritos. A version of the popular "refried" beans that can also be used on nachos.

Four Chalupas. Crisp whole corn tortillas with "refried" beans, lettuce, tomato, onion, jalapeños, and cheese.

Quesadillas. Hot corn tortillas with melted cheese, chopped onion, and peppers.

Jalapeños Rellenos. A stuffed pepper appetizer.

Coctél de Camarón. Shrimp cocktail with a serrano tang.

Sopa de Fideo. Vermicelli simmered with onion, garlic, cumin, and tomatoes.

Arroz Texano. Rice with bits of tomato and a mild cumin and pepper flavor.

Molletes. Mashed black or pinto beans on toasted bolillos with crumbled cheese.

Chilaquiles. Crispy tortilla chips topped with chile verde and crumbled cheese.

LOWFAT TORTILLA CHIPS

For sauce, bean dip, nachos, and chalupas

A number of companies in the United States are now marketing baked tortilla chips for dipping and for making nachos. It takes a bit of practice to bake your own, but after you become accustomed to eating them this way, it will be hard to return to eating fried chips on a regular basis.

Heat the oven to 400°. Place eight corn tortillas on the top rack. You have to watch these closely. After five minutes, remove one and check it for crispness. Remove the tortillas at the slightest hint of browning. Let them cool for a few minutes before serving. You can also cut the tortillas up before baking them. Watch these closely too since they will probably be ready more quickly than the whole tortilla.

If you would like to flavor your chips, wet the tortillas, sprinkle salt, garlic powder, or a little ground cayenne on them and bake.

PEPPERS AND HOT SAUCES

A wide variety of fresh and dried peppers are used to make the many types of sauces used in Mexican cooking. You find cooked and uncooked sauces, very hot sauces, and very mild sauces. Some sauces use the red tomato while others use the small green tomatillo. The selection of sauces you find in this "Hors d'oeuvres and Accompaniments" section is just a small sample of the many types of sauces found throughout Mexico and in restaurants and homes in the United States. Tomato or tomatillo sauces with serranos, jalapeños, or the tiny, very hot piquín peppers, flavored with ground cumin and cilantro, are representative of sauces in the southwestern United States and some parts of Mexico. In New Mexico, the flavor of the green or red pepper itself, without tomatoes, and with minimal additional spices, characterizes the sauce.

The peppers featured in most of the fish, meat, and poultry recipes are fresh jalapeño and serrano peppers. The piquín (or pequín), rarely available commercially, can be substituted for jalapeños or serranos if you are fortunate enough to have a plant that grows these tiny peppers or know someone who does. Anaheim, or California green peppers, ancho peppers, and poblano peppers are other peppers called for in recipes for green enchiladas and menudo. "Bell" peppers refer to the mild green peppers often used in stuffed pepper recipes.

A chipotle sauce recipe and chipotle chicken recipe are included to demonstrate the very unusual smoky flavor of the chipotle pepper. The sauce can be used as a dip or as a sauce for meat or chicken. Whole chipotle peppers can be added to a pot of black or pinto beans for a hotter version of the bean soup recipe included in this book.

Most hot sauce recipes included here are written for the blender or food processor. For fresh peppers and tomatoes, using a "molcajete" is ideal for producing a sauce that is unparalleled in flavor and aroma. The molcajete is a stone mortar traditionally used for mashing peppers, onion, garlic, tomatoes, and spices into the wide variety of tastes you find in Mexican sauces. The mashing effect of the stone against the fresh ingredients seems to release and blend the flavors more so than when ingredients are just mixed together. Molcajetes are highly recommended and, fortunately, are becoming available in many parts of the United States.

If you use a blender or food processor to make sauces, use it for only a few seconds at a time. Cut the ingredients into small pieces, add the liquids and spices, and blend for five seconds at a time to avoid producing a runny sauce with indistinguishable ingredients. At times when you do want a very smooth consistency, a blender or food processor is indispensable. For example, a smooth tomatillo sauce and sauces made from dried red peppers, anchos, and chipotles are best made in the blender or food processor.

As you prepare the ingredients for making sauce, you may want to consider removing the seeds from the peppers before blending. This is all a matter of taste, but when you do remove seeds, keep in mind that the seeds and peppers can be slightly irritating to sensitive skin. As another precaution, always allow food to cool sufficiently before blending. This avoids the possibility of being burned by hot liquids or steam escaping from the blender or food processor.

Regardless of the type of sauce you make, whether cooked or raw, red or green, in a molcajete, food processor, or blender, your imagination is always the only limit to the endless flavors and textures of the many types of Mexican hot sauces.

SALSA PICOSA DE TOMATE Y CHILE
Spicy Tomato and Pepper Sauce

2 Cups

4 small tomatoes, chopped
4 serrano or jalapeño peppers, chopped
1 garlic clove, chopped
1 very small onion or part of a medium onion, chopped
1/4 teaspoon ground cumin
1/4 teaspoon black pepper
1 teaspoon diced carrot
2 tablespoons or more water if needed for desired consistency
Dash of garlic powder
Salt and black pepper to taste
Cilantro; a few chopped leaves can be added after the other ingredients are blended.

Procedures

Chop the tomatoes, peppers, garlic clove, and onion, and place them into the blender or food processor. Add spices, diced carrot, and water.

Blend for five seconds.

Add a bit more water if you would like the sauce to be thinner. There is no right or wrong in consistency. A touch of tarragon vinegar can smooth out an extremely spicy sauce and make it a bit more palatable.

Run the blender for another five seconds and pour the mixture into a serving dish. Add additional salt, pepper, and cumin if desired. Top with chopped cilantro leaves.

Serving Suggestions

Cooked Red Sauce
Simmer the tomatoes, onion, garlic, carrot, and peppers in a saucepan for about twenty minutes or until the tomatoes and peppers are very soft. Add other ingredients, blend, and serve.

SALSA DE TOMATILLO Y CHILE
Tomatillo (green tomatoes) and Green Pepper Sauce

This tomatillo sauce is green and smooth with a tangy flavor that
is quite different from the red tomato sauces. Tomatillos should
be simmered and softened for five or ten minutes before you use
them.

2 Cups

        6 tomatillos
      1/2 small onion, chopped
        4 medium serranos, chopped
        1 garlic clove, chopped
      1/4 teaspoon ground cumin
        2 tablespoons water
        2 tablespoons chopped cilantro
           Salt and black pepper to taste

Procedures

Remove the outer covers and stems from the tomatillos and
wash them thoroughly with warm water. Place them in a sauce
pan with water and simmer for five to ten minutes.

Place the tomatillos and all the other ingredients in the blender
or food processor. Blend until the sauce reaches the desired
consistency. Add a tablespoon or two of water if needed. Top
with additional chopped cilantro leaves.

Serving Suggestions

This is very similar to the green sauce included later for green
enchiladas. The major difference is in the use of Anaheim
peppers for the enchilada sauce. Anaheim peppers are milder
than serranos and more suitable for use in an enchilada sauce.

NEW MEXICO RED PEPPER SAUCE

This sauce is made with the red New Mexico peppers that are dried in decorative bundles called "ristras." Ristras are sold throughout New Mexico and Texas, particularly during the December holiday season. This pepper also forms the basis for the sauce in "Enchiladas Las Cruces."

2 Cups

- 8 large New Mexico red peppers
- 1 medium onion, chopped
- 1 garlic clove, chopped
- 1 cup of water; in addition to water used for simmering the peppers
  Salt and black pepper to taste

Procedures

Cover the peppers with water in a saucepan and simmer for twenty minutes with half of the chopped onion and the garlic clove. Drain the water and remove the peppers to cool. Discard the onion and garlic.

After the peppers have cooled sufficiently to handle safely, remove the stems, slice the peppers lengthwise, and remove the seeds from inside the peppers.

Place the peppers, 1/2 cup of water, and the remainder of the chopped onion in a blender. A food processor is not quite as effective for liquefying the peppers.

Blend thoroughly until the peppers, water, and onion form a smooth mixture. Add water to reach a consistency suitable for sauce.

Pour the sauce through a strainer to remove remaining seeds and bits of pepper.

Serving Suggestions

The sauce can be spiced up a bit more with garlic powder, ground cumin, and salt.

PICO DE GALLO

2 Cups

   2 large tomatoes
   4 jalapeño or serrano peppers
   1 medium onion
   2 garlic cloves
 1/4 cup cilantro
 1/2 tablespoon black pepper
   4 tablespoons cold water
   1 tablespoon white wine vinegar or tarragon vinegar
      Juice of 1 lime
      Salt to taste

Procedures

On a large cutting surface, cut tomatoes, peppers, onion, and garlic into small pieces. Chop and blend all the ingredients together with the knife to assure a nice blending of flavors. Add the cilantro, black pepper, and salt, and continue to chop the ingredients, mixing them all on the same cutting surface.

Place all the ingredients into a serving bowl and add the water and vinegar. Plain vinegar or another flavored vinegar can also be used in this recipe.

Squeeze the juice from the lime into the mixture and stir several times before serving.

Serving Suggestions

Pico de Gallo should be very spicy with a hint of vinegar and lime and plenty of black pepper. You can serve this with chips, in quesadillas, and with a main course. Experiment with the number of peppers and tomatoes and with the vinegar-water-lime mixture to suit your tastes.

CHIPOTLE SAUCE

1/2 Cup

4 chipotle peppers
1/2 medium onion, chopped
2 garlic cloves, chopped
1/4 cup of water
 Dash of cumin
 Salt and black pepper to taste

Procedures

If you use dried chipotle peppers, break them open and remove as many of the seeds as you can. Simmer the peppers for ten minutes in water to clean and soften them prior to using. Drain the water and let the peppers cool.

Place the peppers into a blender or food processor. Add the water and all other ingredients and blend until the sauce is very smooth. Flavor with additional salt and cumin if desired and add a few tablespoons of water for an extra smooth consistency.

Serving Suggestions

Chipotle peppers can also be used to make a sauce for chicken or beef dishes. See the "Pollo en Salsa Chipotle" recipe for a variation of this sauce.

BASIC NACHOS

24 Nachos

6 corn tortillas

2 ounces reduced-fat cheddar cheese (5 grams of fat per ounce), grated

4-6 small serrano or jalapeño peppers (fresh or pickled), sliced

1 small tomato, finely chopped

1 small onion, finely chopped

Procedures

Cut each tortilla into four pieces. Place the pieces on a baking sheet and bake for about five minutes in a 400° oven until slightly brown and crisp.

Arrange the tortilla chips close together on a pie dish, cookie sheet, or pan, with the sides of the chips touching.

Distribute the cheese, onion, and peppers on the chips. Top with finely chopped tomato.

Place the nachos into a 400° oven and heat until the cheese begins to melt (about five minutes).

Microwave oven

Arrange the baked tortilla chips on a pie dish or platter designed for use in the microwave oven.

Top the chips with cheese, onion, peppers, and tomatoes.

Microwave for one minute on HIGH. The cheese should just be beginning to melt at the end of one minute. Add another thirty seconds cooking time if necessary.

Serve immediately.

Serving Suggestions

Nachos can go way beyond basic by spreading the chips with "refried" beans before adding cheese and the other toppings (see "Frijoles Refritos"). Cooked chicken breast or small amounts of beef can also be added. Other suggestions include using small amounts of lowfat sour cream as a topping for the nachos.

FRIJOLES REFRITOS
"Fried" Beans

A lowfat version of the "refried" beans served in Mexican restaurants can be made simply by heating whole pinto beans and mashing them thoroughly (see "Frijoles Charros" recipe). If you consider the canned beans carried in many grocery stores, check labels to avoid buying refried or whole beans cooked with lard or other fat.

This is a versatile way to use leftover whole beans. You can make bean tacos, burritos, nachos with beans, or have them as a side dish on a plate of enchiladas.

Procedures

Heat cooked whole pinto beans in a pan and mash until smooth. For every two cups of whole beans, include 1/2 cup of the water used for cooking the beans.

Simmer on low heat, stirring occasionally, until the mixture thickens. Add a tablespoon or two of water if needed to achieve the desired consistency. The beans are ready when they can be spread on a baked corn tortilla chip for nachos or on whole baked corn tortillas for chalupas.

For a spicier flavor, add a finely chopped pepper, a bit of minced onion and garlic, and a few leaves of fresh cilantro before mashing. Other flavors can be added with tomato, cayenne, garlic powder, or any number of other seasonings.

For nachos with beans, spread the thickened bean mixture on baked corn tortilla chips. Adding beans as the first layer (before the cheese) adds an interesting flavor. In fact, to some folks, "They ain't nachos without beans!"

FOUR CHALUPAS

4 Chalupas

4 corn tortillas
1 cup of whole cooked pinto beans; see "Frijoles Charros"
   recipe.
1 ounce cheddar cheese
2 jalapeño or serrano peppers, pickled or raw; chopped or
   thinly sliced
2 medium tomatoes, chopped
1 small onion, sliced
   Lettuce, enough for four chalupas, chopped

Procedures

Bake corn tortillas in a 400° oven until slightly brown and crisp.
Set aside until they cool enough to handle easily.

Mash enough cooked whole pinto beans for the number of
chalupas you plan to make. One cup of whole beans will
probably suffice for four chalupas. Heat the beans until they are
thick enough to use as a spread on the crisp corn tortillas.

Spread the bean mixture evenly on the crisp tortillas.

Sprinkle grated cheese on the tortillas. Add the remaining
ingredients and serve with hot sauce.

If you want these very hot, you can heat them in the microwave
oven for about a minute on HIGH before you top with lettuce.
This shouldn't be necessary, however, if the beans are very hot
when you spread them.

QUESADILLAS
A Cheese Snack With Very Little Cheese

4 Quesadillas

4 corn tortillas
1 ounce grated cheddar or jack cheese
2 raw or pickled serrano or jalapeño peppers, chopped
1 tomato, chopped
1 small onion, chopped

Procedures

Slightly moisten both sides of the corn tortillas with water.

Heat a tortilla on one side for just about five seconds on a very hot griddle or "comal." Remove the tortilla and add some grated cheese, chopped onion, chopped tomato, and sliced peppers. These are just appetizers so small amounts of the ingredients will suffice. Repeat this with each tortilla.

Lower the heat on the comal to medium and allow the comal to cool slightly before heating the quesadillas.

Place a filled tortilla on the comal for fifteen seconds. After about fifteen seconds, fold it using tongs or a knife while it is on the comal. Pat the quesadilla closed. Turn the quesadilla over and heat the other side for approximately fifteen seconds or until the cheese begins to melt. Repeat this with each quesadilla. Keep them warm in aluminum foil or in a cloth napkin until you are ready to eat them. Reheat them on the comal if necessary.

Microwave oven

Add a small amount of cheese, onion, pepper, and tomato to a slightly moistened corn tortilla. Repeat this with each tortilla. Place the filled tortillas on a dish and microwave for thirty seconds on HIGH. Fold the tortillas in half and microwave for another thirty seconds on HIGH or until the cheese begins to melt. Remove and serve immediately.

Serving Suggestions

These are great snacks for any time of the day or night. If you have corn tortillas that are several days old, they can be "revitalized" by moistening them slightly and microwaving several at one time for about twenty seconds on HIGH.

If your corn tortillas are frozen, they can easily be separated by opening the package and heating the tortillas in the open plastic bag for a minute on HIGH.

Instead of peppers, tomato, and onion, you can simply add a teaspoon of hot sauce you buy or make.

JALAPEÑOS RELLENOS
Stuffed Jalapeños

This is an easy pickled pepper appetizer to make in advance of the dinner and other snacks. Pickled jalapeños tend to be a bit milder than the fresh peppers, probably due to the effect of aging and the vinegar used.

12 Peppers

- 12 whole pickled jalapeño peppers
- 1 ounce lowfat cream cheese spread (2 grams of fat per ounce)
- 1/2 small onion, finely chopped
  Salt and black pepper to taste

Procedures

Slit the peppers lengthwise on one side and carefully remove the seeds from inside. Leave the stems attached.

Add finely chopped onion to the lowfat cream cheese and stir until mixed thoroughly.

Spoon a small amount of cream cheese spread and onion mixture into the open peppers and refrigerate until ready to serve.

COCTEL DE CAMARON
Shrimp Cocktail

This can also be made with canned or bottled tomato sauce or puree for convenience.

    1 lb. shrimp, shelled, deveined, and boiled for five minutes
    4 medium tomatoes, quartered
    1 medium onion, sliced
    1 garlic clove, chopped
3 1/2 cups of water
    1 small serrano, finely chopped
  1/2 teaspoon finely crushed oregano
    2 teaspoons worcestershire sauce
    1 teaspoon horseradish sauce
    1 teaspoon tabasco or red pepper sauce
    1 tablespoon chopped cilantro leaves
      Juice of 1 lemon
      Juice of 1 lime
      Salt and black pepper to taste

Procedures

To make two cups of cocktail sauce, simmer the tomatoes with onion and garlic in three cups of water for forty-five minutes. Remove the skins from the tomatoes as they come loose. Drain the water and allow the tomatoes to cool while you prepare the shrimp. Discard the onion and garlic.

In a pot of boiling water, cook the shrimp for approximately five minutes or until they begin to turn pink. Drain the water and refrigerate the shrimp.

In a blender or food processor, add the cooked tomatoes, 1/2 cup of water, the serrano, oregano, worcestershire sauce, horseradish sauce, red pepper sauce, lemon and lime juice, black pepper and salt. Blend until the sauce is very smooth.

Combine the shrimp and sauce, top with chopped cilantro leaves, and cover. Refrigerate for at least two hours before serving.

Serve with toothpicks or small forks, lime wedges, and tabasco or other spicy sauce.

MOLLETES

Molletes are served for breakfast in Oaxaca and throughout Mexico with steaming cups of café con leche. The cheese that is regularly used in Mexico to top molletes and chilaquiles is a white, semi-dry cheese, often from goat milk, that crumbles easily.

8 Pieces

1 1-lb. loaf of French bread or 4 bolillos
2 cups of "refried" pinto or black beans
1 ounce grated queso blanco, queso fresco, or other mild, white cheese
1 garlic clove, minced

Procedures

Slice a loaf of French bread lengthwise first, then across the pieces, into at least eight pieces. Slice bolillos lengthwise.

Prepare cooked pinto or black beans by heating them thoroughly and mashing them until they reach a smooth consistency. Flavor the beans with garlic and onion to your taste. When the beans have thickened, spread a layer of beans on each piece of bread and sprinkle with grated cheese and bits of garlic.

Place the pieces of bread under a hot broiler for about thirty seconds or until the cheese begins to melt. Remove and serve immediately.

CHILAQUILES

How spicy the chilaquiles are depends on the tomatillo sauce and the amount of jalapeño peppers you use. Chilaquiles are also served as a side dish at breakfast topped with pieces of chicken or dried beef.

16 Chilaquiles

- 4 corn tortillas or 16 lowfat tortilla chips
- 1/2 cup tomatillo sauce
- 1 ounce grated queso blanco
- 1 jalapeño, chopped
- 1/2 medium onion, sliced

Procedures

Prepare the tortilla chips by cutting each corn tortilla into at least four pieces. Bake the pieces of corn tortilla in a 400° oven until they are slightly brown and crisp.

Arrange the baked chips on a flat dish suitable for use in the oven. Heat the tomatillo sauce and spread the sauce evenly on the baked tortilla chips.

Top the chips and tomatillo sauce with the grated cheese, sliced onion, and jalapeño peppers.

Heat the chilaquiles in a 400° oven for five minutes.

Microwave oven

Arrange the chips on a flat dish suitable for the microwave oven. Spread the tomatillo sauce over the chips and top with grated cheese, sliced onion, and jalapeño slices.

Heat on HIGH for one minute or until the cheese begins to melt slightly.

SOPA DE FIDEO
A Vermicelli Side Dish

4 Servings

- 5 ounces dried vermicelli
- 1 teaspoon olive oil
- 2 garlic cloves, chopped
- 1/2 medium onion, chopped
- 1 small tomato, chopped
- 1/2 cup tomato sauce
- 1/2 teaspoon ground cumin
- 2 1/2 cups water
- Salt and black pepper to taste

Procedures

Heat the oil in a pan over medium-high heat. Add the garlic bits, onion, and vermicelli and sauté, stirring constantly. Cook for three to five minutes or until the vermicelli begins to brown slightly.

Add the tomato, tomato sauce, cumin, black pepper, salt, and water. Bring the water to a boil then reduce heat to low setting.

Simmer the fideo for six to eight minutes on low heat or until the fideo begins to get tender ("al dente"). There is no need to cover the fideo while it is simmering. Stir once or twice during the cooking and be careful to avoid overcooking.

Drain most of the water and serve immediately. The fideo should be rather "wet" when served.

Serving Suggestions

Try this with a chopped serrano, jalapeño, or bell pepper. Use cayenne or crushed red pepper flakes for an extra spicy flavor. This is a nice change of pace from rice and it goes with beef and chicken equally well. Chicken broth may be substituted for some of the water.

ARROZ TEXANO
Texas-style Rice

2 Cups

    1 cup of uncooked white rice
    1 teaspoon olive or vegetable oil
  1/2 medium onion, chopped
    2 garlic cloves, chopped
    1 medium tomato, chopped
  1/2 teaspoon ground cumin
  1/4 cup tomato sauce
1 1/2 cups of water
    1 serrano or jalapeño pepper, quartered lengthwise (optional)
       Salt and black pepper to taste

Procedures

Heat the oil. The pot or pan you use should have a tight-fitting lid.

When the oil is hot, add the rice, onion, and garlic. Stir and cook these ingredients until the rice starts to brown.

Add the tomato, cumin, and black pepper. Stir briefly to mix with the rice, onion, and garlic.

Add the tomato sauce. Mix the ingredients. Another half tomato or 1/2 cup of water may be substituted for the tomato sauce.

Add the water and stir once or twice.

Bring the rice mixture to a boil. If you use the serrano or jalapeño pepper, place the pieces of pepper on top of the rice before covering the dish.

Lower heat to low setting and cover.

Cook for twenty-five minutes without lifting the lid. Remove from the heat and let stand for at least ten minutes.

The rice can be reheated nicely in the microwave oven.

Serving Suggestions

Brown rice: Use the same directions and cook on low heat for fifty minutes without lifting the lid. Set aside for at least ten minutes before serving.

If you like your rice redder, add more tomato sauce and proportionately less water until it is as red as you like it. Steamed white rice is served in many places throughout Mexico as well as in Puerto Rico. Occasionally, small peas are added for flavor and decoration.

Soups and Salads

Ensalada de Berro. A mixture of romaine lettuce, fresh onion rings, watercress leaves, and lemon juice.

Cucumber and Jícama Salad. A cool, crispy combination of jícama, cucumber, and lime juice.

Red and Green Pepper Salad. Sweet green and red peppers sprinkled with black pepper.

Asparagus and Pimiento Salad. A lime flavored salad with asparagus and generous portions of pimientos, topped with finely chopped green onion.

Gazpacho. A cool, refreshing soup made with tomatoes, cucumbers, and spices.

Caldo de Pescado. Small pieces of fish simmered with tomatoes, onions, cilantro, peppers, and a variety of spices.

Tortilla Soup. Chicken stock served over crisp corn tortilla strips and garnished with grated cheese.

Caldo de Res. A vegetable and beef breakfast favorite served with a side dish of rice.

Caldo de Pollo. This soup includes a variety of vegetables and is traditionally served with a side dish of rice. Lemon wedges are also brought separately for individual flavoring.

Crab and Corn Soup. A creamy combination of seafood and vegetable flavors.

Lowfat Menudo. This tripe and pepper soup has gained a reputation as a "cure-all" for festive overindulgence and the sleep deprivation that typically accompanies this state.

Frijoles Charros. Bean soup with pinto or black beans, cilantro, tomato, and onion. Served over rice as a complete meal or as a side order to many dishes.

Pozole. A Mexican and New Mexican traditional meal of pork and hominy.

SALADS

Although Mexican food is not particularly noted for salads, many Mexican meals are served with at least a lettuce and tomato garnish. A guacamole salad is often served as an appetizer or as part of the main course in many Mexican restaurants, but because of the very high fat content in avocados, fresh lettuce, chopped tomatoes, fresh onions, peppers, and hot sauce are more highly recommended accompaniments.

ENSALADA DE BERRO
Watercress Salad

Although watercress is delicious with just a drizzle of lemon juice, a tasty salad of your favorite lettuce mixed with watercress can be made easily. This one uses romaine lettuce.

- 1 head of romaine lettuce
- 1 cup watercress
- 1/2 small onion, sliced into rings
    Juice of a lemon
    Salt and black pepper to taste

Procedures

Tear or cut the lettuce leaves into serving sizes and mix with pieces of watercress.

Add onion rings, lemon juice, salt, and black pepper. Mix thoroughly.

Serving Suggestions

Top the salad with a dressing that is popular in Mexico. Mix a small amount of olive oil, water, oregano and mint. We suggest strictly limiting the oil, however, and using more water or substituting lemon juice in your mix.

CUCUMBER AND JICAMA SALAD

1 cup of peeled and sliced cucumbers
1 cup of jícama strips
   Juice of 1 lime
   Dash of cayenne pepper
   Salt and black pepper to taste

Procedures

Peel and slice the cucumbers. Peel the jícama and slice it into thin strips 2" to 3" long. Mix the cucumbers and jícama and sprinkle the lime juice and cayenne pepper over the mixture. Chill for two hours before serving.

Serving Suggestions

VARIATION #1:   This salad can also be made without the cucumber as just a jícama salad.

VARIATION #2:   If you like a more creamy salad, mix in 1/2 cup of plain yogurt, preferably with little or no fat.

RED AND GREEN PEPPER SALAD

1 medium green pepper, sliced
1 medium sweet red pepper, sliced
1 small purple onion, sliced
1/2 cup white wine vinegar
1/2 teaspoon black pepper
   Juice of 1 lemon

Procedures

Cut open the peppers and remove seeds and stems. Slice the peppers into strips. Put the peppers in a salad bowl and add the sliced purple onion. Add the wine vinegar and the lemon juice. Sprinkle with black pepper.

Chill before serving.

ASPARAGUS AND PIMIENTO SALAD

Asparagus (as much as you would like to eat)
1/2 cup of sliced sweet pimientos
1 bunch of green onions, finely chopped
Juice of 1 lime
Salt and black pepper to taste

Procedures

Cut the asparagus into 1" to 2" strips. Steam the asparagus with a few tablespoons of water in a microwave oven (preferably) until tender, but not soft. Add the pimientos and onions and drizzle with the lime juice. Season with salt and black pepper and serve with additional pieces of lime.

GAZPACHO

Cold Tomato Soup

Four 4-oz. Servings

1 small onion, chopped
2 cloves garlic, chopped
1 teaspoon lemon juice
1/3 cup green pepper (bell pepper), chopped
4 medium tomatoes, chopped
1 bunch green onions, finely chopped
1 large cucumber, peeled and chopped
2 cups tomato juice
1/2 teaspoon crushed oregano
1/4 teaspoon tabasco or red pepper sauce
2 tablespoons white wine vinegar
Salt and black pepper to taste

Procedures

Make the first three ingredients (onion, garlic, lemon juice) into a paste using a molcajete, blender, or food processor. Combine all other ingredients and mix in the paste until it is completely dissolved.

Cover and chill the gazpacho in a glass bowl for three hours. Serve with fresh cilantro and diced green onion.

TORTILLA SOUP

4 Cups

6 corn tortillas
1 small onion, chopped
1 clove garlic, very finely chopped
1 serrano pepper, finely chopped
4 carrots, cut into very thin strips (about 1" long)
2 cups water
2 cups of chicken broth
2 ounces grated jack cheese
   Salt and black pepper to taste
   Cilantro leaves, chopped

Procedures

Cut the tortillas into 1/4" thin strips (1" to 2" long) and bake at 400° until slightly brown and crisp.

Simmer onion, garlic, serrano pepper, carrots, water, and chicken broth for thirty minutes. Season with salt and pepper to taste.

To serve, put a portion of the crisp tortillas strips into the bottom of each serving bowl. Pour the soup over the top. Top with a small amount of jack cheese. Serve cilantro leaves and finely chopped serrano pepper for extra flavoring.

CALDO DE PESCADO
Fish Soup

4 Cups

1/2 pound red snapper fillets cut into 2" pieces
  1 cup diced celery
  2 tomatoes, quartered
  1 medium onion, chopped
  1 teaspoon crushed oregano
  1 serrano pepper, chopped
  2 bay leaves
  2 cloves garlic, chopped
  4 cups water
1/2 cup cilantro, chopped
  2 green onions, finely chopped

Procedures

Put tomatoes, onion, garlic into a molcajete, blender, or food processor and blend to make into a smooth liquid. Put this liquid into a pot, add the water, bay leaves, celery, oregano, and serrano pepper and bring to a boil. Lower the heat and simmer the liquid for ten minutes, allowing the ingredients to flavor the broth.

Add the fish and simmer for ten minutes. Stir the soup gently once or twice taking care to avoid breaking the fish apart.

Serve fish and broth into each bowl and top with cilantro and chopped green onions. Include bread and lemon wedges as accompaniments.

CRAB AND CORN SOUP

4 Cups

4 ears fresh sweet corn
2 tomatoes, quartered
1 onion, chopped
1 garlic clove, finely chopped
1 cup shredded crab meat
4 cups water
4 tablespoons nonfat yogurt
   Dash of tabasco or other red sauce to taste
   Cilantro garnish

Procedures

Cut the corn off the cob. Put half of the corn, the tomatoes, onion, and garlic into a soup pan with the water. Bring to a boil. Reduce heat and stir in the yogurt slowly. Cover and simmer for one hour.

Add the remainder of the corn, dashes of tabasco, and crab. Simmer for twenty more minutes. Serve with cilantro garnish.

CALDO DE POLLO
Chicken Soup

4 Bowls

  1 chicken, quartered, with skin removed
  8 cups water for initial boiling of chicken
 12 cups of water for final preparation of soup
  2 garlic cloves, chopped
  2 bay leaves
  1 whole jalapeño, punctured with a fork once or twice
  1 onion, sliced
  1 turnip, sliced
  1 large tomato, chopped
1/2 cup of fresh cilantro
  6 carrots, cut into large pieces
1/2 head of cabbage, cut into four pieces
  2 large ears of corn, each cut into four pieces
  2 large zucchinis, each cut into eight pieces
  2 jalapeños, quartered lengthwise
  1 teaspoon ground cumin
1/2 teaspoon cayenne pepper
    Juice of one lemon
    Salt and black pepper to taste

Procedures

Cook the chicken for thirty minutes in eight cups of water with one whole garlic clove, one bay leaf, and one whole jalapeño. Add more water if needed to cover the chicken while cooking. Keep the pot covered and stir occasionally.

After thirty minutes, drain the water and rinse the pot clean. Replace the cooked chicken with at least twelve cups of water and add all the remaining ingredients.

Cover and simmer for one hour or until the vegetables are cooked to your liking.

Serving Suggestions

Serve with a side portion of rice, lemon wedges, hot corn tortillas, and hot sauce.

CALDO DE RES
Beef Soup

This is a popular weekend breakfast in many Mexican restaurants throughout Texas and the southwestern United States. Like the caldo de pollo, it is served with a side dish of rice, some lemon wedges, and corn tortillas. The most commonly used pieces of beef are ordinary soup bones with small chunks of beef attached. Top round steak is used in this recipe.

4 Bowls

1	pound top round steak
2	teaspoons olive oil
8	cups of water for initial cooking
12	cups of water for final preparation of soup
3	cloves of garlic, chopped
1	large onion, chopped
2	tomatoes, quartered
1/2	cup fresh cilantro
4	carrots, sliced
1/2	head of cabbage, cut into four pieces
2	zucchinis or other type of squash, sliced
2	jalapeño or serrano peppers, sliced
2	large ears of corn, each cut into four pieces
2	teaspoons ground cumin
1	teaspoon black pepper
	Juice of 1/2 lemon
	Salt to taste

Procedures

Cut all the visible fat from the meat. Cut the meat into soup-size pieces. Brown the meat for ten minutes in the olive oil with one clove of garlic and half of the onion.

After the meat has browned, drain the meat of all liquids, discard the garlic and onion, and place the meat into a large pot. Add eight cups of water to the pot, cover, and cook the meat on medium heat for thirty minutes.

After thirty minutes, drain the water completely from the pot, rinse the pot clean, replace the meat, and add twelve cups of water to the clean pot. Add the remaining garlic and onion, the tomatoes, cilantro, carrots, cabbage, squash, peppers, corn, cumin, and black pepper. Stir in the juice of half a lemon. Simmer for one hour or until the meat and vegetables are cooked to your liking.

Serving Suggestions

Serve with rice, lemon wedges, chopped onion, and fresh chopped cilantro.

You will find many variations of the recipe including the addition of a variety of squashes, beans, etc. Personalize your caldo with your favorite vegetables.

Add jalapeños, cayenne, or tabasco for a very spicy soup.

LOWFAT MENUDO
Tripe Soup

8 Bowls

- 3 pounds of tripe, defrosted, with all visible fat removed
- 5 large New Mexico red peppers or cascabel peppers
- 8 pods ancho peppers
- 1/2 cup of water; in addition to water used for cooking the tripe
- 4 garlic cloves, chopped
- 2 lemons, sliced
- 3 bay leaves
- 1/2 cup cilantro, chopped
- 4 tablespoons crushed oregano
- 1 tablespoon ground cumin
- 1 tablespoon cayenne pepper
- 1 large onion, chopped
- 4 cups yellow or white hominy
  Salt and black pepper to taste

Procedures

If you have purchased frozen tripe, remove all the visible chunks of fat and place the tripe into a large pot of boiling water. Add two bay leaves and several slices of lemon and onion. Frozen or defrosted, the tripe is much easier to cut after it has boiled for an hour or so. Boiling also removes much of the fat that you cannot see prior to cooking. Boil the tripe for an hour to remove the fat.

While the tripe boils, place the red peppers and ancho peppers in a separate pot with water and simmer them for thirty minutes or until tender. Drain the water, remove the stems from the peppers, and let the peppers cool for a few minutes before proceeding.

Put the peppers into a blender or food processor with half a chopped onion, 1/2 cup water, and a dash of salt. Blend until completely smooth. Strain the mixture to remove the seeds and remaining bits of pepper. Set the strained sauce aside until ready for use. NOTE: This sauce is excellent for dipping with chips.

Take the pieces of tripe from the water one by one and cut them into bite-size pieces, removing all the visible fat as you cut.

Discard the water used for boiling the tripe. Rinse the tripe in several changes of water or in a colander until the water drains clear and is relatively free of any visible pieces of fat.

Add the tripe and the pepper sauce to a large pot with fresh water. Add the garlic and several slices of lemon. Add bay leaves, cilantro, a tablespoon of crushed oregano, a tablespoon of ground cumin, the cayenne, and onion. The water should cover the tripe by at least four inches.

Cover and simmer for at least three hours or until the tripe is tender.

Add the hominy, the remaining oregano, and cook for an additional thirty minutes to an hour.

Serving Suggestions

During the cooking process, skim the top of the liquid of any visible oils that accumulate. The initial cooking and draining of the original liquid removes large amounts of hidden fat in the tripe. Traditionally, pigs' feet or ham hocks are also included in the menudo. This, of course, is all a matter of personal taste.

Season the soup with the ingredients listed until the combination of spices and flavors is perfect for you. The quantities shown are usually just starting points with adjustments made as the cooking progresses.

A seasoning for a bowl of menudo can be made by taking equal parts of the following spices and crushing them together and sprinkling on the soup: ground cumin (start with 1/2 teaspoon), ground oregano, ground cayenne, ground red pepper flakes (such as those used on pizza), garlic powder, salt, and black pepper.

Serve with lemon, fresh cilantro, chopped jalapeño, and onion.

FRIJOLES CHARROS

Pinto and black beans are most commonly cooked in this manner. Beans can be cooked one day and eaten for the next couple of days or they can be frozen for longer term storage.

12 cups

  2 lbs. whole dry pinto or black beans
 14 cups water
1/4 cup cilantro, chopped
  1 medium tomato, sliced
  1 large serrano or jalapeño pepper, sliced
  1 small onion, sliced
  1 tablespoon worcestershire sauce
  1 teaspoon black pepper
  2 bay leaves
  1 garlic clove, chopped
     Salt to taste

Procedures

Inspect dry beans carefully for rocks and dirt and wash them thoroughly before placing in a pot with at least a four-quart capacity. Fill the pot with water and turn the heat to medium-high. Add all the ingredients and cover with a tight-fitting lid. Lower the heat to low. If the pot boils over, crack the lid slightly until you know the water will not boil over when the lid is on completely. When possible, replace the lid completely.

Cook the beans for at least four hours and preferably for six. They should be stirred at least every thirty minutes. Keep a close check on the water level, adding water as needed, to keep the water level at least two inches above the beans. No water should be added during the last hour of cooking, so add about two cups of water when the beans are almost done and let them cook for another hour.

Serving Suggestions

Add another tomato if you like the soup slightly thicker. When the beans are cooked, serve them with sliced onion and chopped cilantro.

POZOLE

4 Servings

  1 lb. lean pork loin center, cut into small 1/4" square pieces
12 cups of water
  4 cups yellow or white hominy
  4 medium tomatoes, chopped
  2 medium carrots, finely chopped
  3 serrano peppers, finely chopped
  2 garlic cloves, finely chopped
  2 bay leaves
1/2 teaspoon cayenne
    Juice of 1 lime
    Salt and black pepper to taste

Garnish

10 radishes, diced   2 limes, cut into wedges
 8 green onions, diced   1 ounce queso blanco
 2 cups leaf lettuce, diced

Seasoning

1/2 teaspoon each of red pepper flakes, cumin, oregano, garlic powder, cayenne, and black pepper. Crush all these ingredients together to use as a seasoning for a bowl of pozole.

Procedures

Bring six cups of water to a boil. Add the pork, one bay leaf, one serrano pepper, one garlic clove, and one chopped tomato. Reduce heat to low and simmer for thirty minutes.

Drain the water from the pot. Add six new cups of water to the pot, replace the pork, add hominy, three chopped tomatoes, carrots, two serrano peppers, a garlic clove, bay leaf, cayenne, and black pepper. Add the juice from one lime. Cover and simmer on low heat for one hour.

Serving Suggestions

Suit your tastes with more or fewer serranos, and more or less cayenne, black pepper, and other spices used for seasoning.

When you are ready to serve the pozole, dice radishes, green onions, and lettuce. Serve with wedges of lime, grated cheese, and the powdered seasoning.

An Enchilada Variety

The Basic Enchilada Sauce. Includes directions for making green and red enchilada sauce.

Enchiladas Perfectas. General procedures for making most of the varieties of enchiladas in this section.

Preparing a Chicken Enchilada Filling. Instructions for making a filling for chicken enchiladas; also applicable to other fillings.

Enchiladas de Pollo. Chicken enchiladas, served with red enchilada sauce.

Enchiladas Verdes de Queso. Cheese enchiladas covered with green tomatillo sauce.

Tex-Mex Enchiladas. Texas' most popular and most frequently found on menus, smothered in chile con carne (spicy ground beef).

Enchiladas de Jaiba.   Crab enchiladas, a seafood-enchilada crossover.

Enchiladas Las Cruces. Stacked, unrolled, and served with New Mexico-style red sauce.

GENERAL COMMENTS ABOUT THE ENCHILADA

The enchilada is one of the most versatile foods you'll ever have the pleasure of cooking. Enchiladas are made in a variety of ways throughout the United States and Northern Mexico. Some are rolled, others stacked, and still others folded in half, layered with cheese and onion, and baked in the oven. The enchilada opens up new worlds of possibilities for creative cooking. Crab, shrimp, beef, pork, chicken, turkey, and cheese are just a few of the fillings that are possible with the enchilada!

This section takes you step by step through the process of making enchiladas: making a red and green sauce from tomatoes or tomatillos, filling and rolling cheese enchiladas, and preparing a chicken enchilada filling. These basic steps are then adapted to make "Enchiladas de Pollo," "Enchiladas Verdes de Queso," "Tex-Mex Enchiladas," and "Enchiladas de Jaiba."

THE BASIC ENCHILADA SAUCE

Red Enchilada Sauce

- 8 New Mexico red peppers or cascabel peppers
- 2 ancho peppers
- 4 medium tomatoes, chopped
- 1/2 onion, chopped
- 1 garlic clove, chopped
- 1/2 tablespoon cayenne
- 2 tablespoons oregano
- 1 tablespoon ground cumin
- 1 1/2 cups of water or chicken broth (in addition to water used in initial simmering of peppers)
- 1 tablespoon flour
- 1/4 cup of water for dissolving flour
  Salt and black pepper to taste

Procedures

Simmer the peppers and tomatoes in water for at least thirty minutes or until they are very soft and the stems come off the peppers easily. Discard the water and remove the stems and seeds from the peppers after the peppers have cooled sufficiently.

Place the peppers and half of the water or broth into a blender or food processor. Blend into a very smooth liquid. Pour this liquid through a strainer to remove remaining seeds and bits of pepper. Pour the blended peppers and liquid back into the blender.

Add the tomatoes, onion, garlic, cayenne, oregano, cumin, salt, and black pepper into the blender or food processor with the blended peppers and liquid. Blend all the ingredients into a very smooth sauce. Add the remainder of the water or broth and pour all the mixture into a large saucepan.

Dissolve the flour in 1/4 cup of water and add to the saucepan. Stir the sauce several times, cover, and simmer this mixture for at least thirty minutes on low heat. It should begin to reach a gravy-like consistency in about thirty to forty-five minutes. Add cooking time if the mixture has not thickened satisfactorily within forty-five minutes. Add a tablespoon or two of water if the mixture thickens too rapidly.

Spice to taste before serving with enchiladas.

Green Enchilada Sauce

- 5   large Anaheim peppers
- 6   tomatillos
- 1   medium onion, chopped
- 2   garlic cloves, chopped
- 2   teaspoons ground cumin
- 4   serranos (or more), chopped
- 1   teaspoon cayenne
- 1   cup water—or chicken broth if you're making chicken enchiladas
- 1/2   cup water for dissolving flour
- 1   tablespoon flour
    Salt and black pepper to taste

Procedures

Remove the covers and stems from the tomatillos and place the tomatillos and whole peppers in a large saucepan. Cover the tomatillos and peppers with water.

Add half of the chopped onion and one garlic clove and simmer on low heat for twenty-five minutes or until the peppers and tomatillos are soft.

Discard the water, onion, and garlic used in simmering and allow the peppers and tomatillos to cool for a few minutes.

Remove the stems from the peppers and slice them lengthwise to remove as many seeds as possible.

Put the tomatillos and peppers into the food processor or blender with 1/2 cup of water or chicken broth (for chicken enchiladas). Blend until a smooth sauce is formed. Pour the sauce through a strainer to remove the remaining tomatillo seeds. Pour the strained sauce back into the blender or food processor.

Add chopped onion, fresh garlic, ground cumin, chopped serranos, cayenne, and a dash of black pepper to the sauce. Add salt to taste. Blend again until very smooth. Pour the blended sauce into a saucepan and add 1/2 cup of water or chicken broth (for chicken enchiladas).

Dissolve the flour in 1/4 cup of water and add this to the saucepan.

Cover and simmer for thirty to forty-five minutes on low heat, stirring occasionally while the mixture thickens. Add cayenne, cumin, salt, or serranos for extra spiciness. Add cooking time if needed or a tablespoon or two of water if the sauce thickens very rapidly.

ENCHILADAS PERFECTAS

Enchiladas are usually made by dipping corn tortillas in oil before filling and rolling. The oil keeps the corn tortillas from falling apart during cooking and makes it possible to reheat the leftovers. These enchiladas are made without the oil. Therefore, it probably is best to make only as many as you will eat in one meal. The sauce should be spooned over the enchiladas only after they have been heated thoroughly in the oven.

This recipe, made with only a cheese and onion filling, serves as the basis for "Enchiladas de Pollo," "Enchiladas Verdes de Queso," "Tex-Mex Enchiladas," and "Enchiladas de Jaiba."

Substitute the cheese and onion used as the filling in this recipe with the filling of your choice. You will need to prepare the sauce in advance of the enchilada preparation. Enchiladas are extremely versatile and can be filled with a variety of food not shown here.

12 Enchiladas

  12 corn tortillas
    4 ounces grated cheddar or jack cheese
    2 cups enchilada sauce
    1 medium onion, chopped
1-2 jalapeño or serrano peppers, chopped; optional
1/2 teaspoon vegetable oil for baking dish.

Procedures

Cover the bottom and sides of the dish you will use for baking with about 1/2 teaspoon of vegetable oil. If you plan to use the microwave oven, make sure your dish is safe for the microwave oven.

Combine half of the grated cheese and half of the chopped onion. Divide the cheese and onion combination into twelve small portions. These enchiladas tend to be better if you use only small amounts of filling in each so that you can roll the tortilla fairly tightly.

Heat the comal or griddle on high heat.

Moisten a corn tortilla with water and heat it on the hot comal until it is very hot and flexible. Add a portion of cheese and onion to the tortilla and roll it up.

Place the rolled tortilla with the seam down on the oiled baking dish.

Repeat the heating, filling, and rolling until all the tortillas are filled and placed next to each other in the baking dish.

Top the assembled enchiladas with the remainder of the grated cheese and chopped onion. Add chopped serrano or jalapeño peppers if desired.

Heat, uncovered, in a 400° oven for six to eight minutes or until the cheese just begins to bubble.

Remove and serve with green or red enchilada sauce.

Microwave oven

Fill and roll each enchilada using the procedures described above. After topping the enchiladas with cheese, onion, and peppers, place them into the microwave oven and heat for five minutes on HIGH.

Serve immediately with green or red enchilada sauce.

Serving Suggestions

The sauce should be spooned over each serving of enchiladas only after they have been heated thoroughly in the oven. This will prevent them from getting soaked and falling apart during the heating. Make only as many enchiladas as you will eat in one meal. Rice, beans, hot sauce, and corn tortillas always make nice accompaniments to enchiladas.

PREPARING A CHICKEN ENCHILADA FILLING

2 Cups

  1 lb. chicken breast
1/2 tablespoon olive or vegetable oil
  1 medium onion, chopped
2-3 garlic cloves, chopped
  1 small jalapeño or serrano pepper, chopped (optional)
1/2 cup water or chicken broth
  1 teaspoon ground cumin
1/2 teaspoon cayenne or chile powder
1/2 teaspoon crushed oregano
1/2 teaspoon garlic powder
1/2 teaspoon paprika
1/2 teaspoon black pepper
   Salt to taste

Procedures

Remove the skin and bone from the chicken. Cut the chicken into pieces slightly less than one-inch square. Heat 1/2 tablespoon of vegetable, olive, or other preferred oil in a skillet. Add the chicken, a chopped onion, two or three chopped garlic cloves, and a chopped jalapeño or serrano pepper. Stir while the mixture is cooking and browning.

Add 1/2 cup of water (or chicken broth) when the chicken, onions, and garlic begin to brown.

Spice the mixture with 1/2 teaspoon each of ground cumin, chili powder or cayenne, oregano, garlic powder, paprika, and black pepper. Don't worry about exact measurements (except for the peppers and chili powder or cayenne!).

Lower the heat, cover, and simmer for about thirty minutes. At the end of this period, stir the mixture, and check to see if the chicken is cooked (it should be) and broken up enough to roll into a corn tortilla. At this point, if you aren't quite ready to proceed with the actual filling, rolling, and baking the enchiladas, add a bit more water and continue simmering on low. The spices will continue to blend nicely and the mixture will become even softer and easier to use in enchiladas. Keep an eye on the liquid level of the mixture. You should keep at least a fourth of a cup of liquid in the mixture throughout the simmering.

Microwave oven

After removing the bone and skin from the chicken breasts, cut the chicken into small pieces. Place the chicken pieces and 1/4 cup of water or chicken broth into a baking dish suitable for the microwave oven. Cover and microwave for twelve minutes on HIGH. Let stand for at least two minutes before removing. Drain the liquid from the baking dish.

Add another 1/4 cup of water or broth and all other ingredients (except oil) to the baking dish. Cover and bake for another twelve minutes on HIGH. Let stand for at least two minutes before opening the dish and stirring the chicken mixture.

After stirring, determine if the mixture is ready to use as a filling. If the chicken still needs to be softened to avoid torn tortillas, add a bit more liquid, and microwave an additional four or five minutes on HIGH.

Serving Suggestions

Regardless of the filling, the principle for preparing it is the same: simmer the meat, chicken, crab, vegetables, or cheese mixture with spices and a bit of liquid, in this case water, until the mixture can be spooned into a tortilla. If you use beef other than ground beef, it should be cut into bite-size pieces and browned slightly before adding the spices and simmering in water or broth.

There is hardly anything you can do wrong when preparing an enchilada filling. Experiment with the assortment of spices, and particularly the amount of spice you use in the mixture.

This is an excellent way to use leftover barbecued chicken.

ENCHILADAS DE POLLO
Chicken Enchiladas

12 Enchiladas

12 corn tortillas
    Chicken Enchilada Filling
 2 cups red enchilada sauce
 4 ounces grated cheddar or jack cheese
1/2 medium onion, sliced
 2 serrano or jalapeño peppers, sliced
1/2 teaspoon oil for baking dish

Procedures

Prepare the filling using directions from "Preparing a Chicken Enchilada Mixture." Leftover barbecued chicken usually works fine too. Add a small portion of the filling to a corn tortilla that has been moistened and heated until flexible. Fill and roll each tortilla and assemble them in a slightly oiled baking dish according to directions for "Enchiladas Perfectas." Top the assembled enchiladas with grated cheese, sliced onion, and sliced jalapeño or serrano peppers.

Heat the enchiladas, uncovered, in a 400° oven for six to eight minutes or until the cheese just begins to bubble.

Remove and top each serving with red enchilada sauce and additional sliced onion and peppers if desired.

Microwave oven

After filling, rolling, and placing the enchiladas in a slightly oiled baking dish, heat for five minutes on HIGH.

Serve with enchilada sauce. Additional topping with onions and peppers is optional.

ENCHILADAS VERDES DE QUESO
Green Cheese Enchiladas

Enchiladas verdes are among the more popular enchiladas served in Texas. This recipe combines directions and ingredients for making cheese enchiladas ("Enchiladas Perfectas") and green enchilada sauce. Chicken can also be used instead of the cheese and onion inside the tortilla.

12 Enchiladas

        12 corn tortillas
         4 ounces grated cheddar or jack cheese
         2 cups enchilada sauce
         1 medium onion, chopped
       1-2 jalapeño or serrano peppers, sliced; optional
       1/2 teaspoon oil for baking dish

Procedures

Prepare green enchilada sauce.

Following directions from "Enchiladas Perfectas," heat each moistened corn tortilla, fill with small portions of cheese and onion, and roll. Half of the cheese will be used as a filling and the other half as a topping.

Assemble the rolled tortillas in a slightly oiled dish suitable for baking in either the conventional or microwave oven. Top with remaining cheese, additional onions, and peppers if desired.

Heat in a 400° oven for six to eight minutes or until the cheese topping begins to melt and bubble. Remove and serve with green enchilada sauce.

Microwave oven

Place the baking dish with the enchiladas in the microwave oven and heat on HIGH for five minutes or until the cheese begins to melt and the enchiladas are obviously very hot. Serve with green enchilada sauce.

Serving Suggestions

These can also be made using the "Enchiladas de Pollo" recipe and the green enchilada sauce.

Other suggestions for serving include the use of a small amount of lowfat sour cream as a topping and a sprinkling of queso blanco to top off the green sauce. Serve with rice, beans, hot sauce, and a garnish of shredded lettuce and chopped tomato.

TEX-MEX ENCHILADAS

In about nine out of ten Mexican restaurants in Texas, this enchilada is usually the standard. "Tex-Mex" enchiladas are traditionally served with generous amounts of beef, cheddar cheese, and onion. You will never find jack cheese or other white cheeses in a genuine Tex-Mex enchilada. Your order will arrive covered with chile con carne, the ingredient that truly makes them Tex-Mex. To make these enchiladas, combine the "Enchiladas Perfectas" recipe with the "Chile con Carne" recipe.

12 Enchiladas

- 12 corn tortillas
- 4 ounces grated cheddar cheese
- 2 cups chile con carne
- 1 medium onion, chopped
- 1-2 jalapeño or serrano peppers, chopped; optional
- 1/2 teaspoon oil for the baking dish

Procedures

Prepare the chile con carne. If you are using chile con carne made on a previous day, heat it prior to using it in this recipe.

Assemble the cheese enchiladas using the "Enchiladas Perfectas" recipe. Half of the cheese and onion should be used for the filling and half for the topping.

Place the rolled tortillas with seam side down in a slightly oiled baking dish.

Top the enchiladas with the remaining half of the cheese and onion. Using additional onions and peppers as a topping is optional.

Bake in a 400° oven for six to eight minutes or until the cheese begins to melt.

Remove the enchiladas from the oven and top each enchilada with two or three tablespoons of chile con carne.

Microwave oven

After preparing the rolled tortillas and placing them in a slightly oiled baking dish suitable for the microwave oven, heat uncovered for five minutes on HIGH.

Remove the enchiladas and spoon chile con carne over each serving.

ENCHILADAS DE JAIBA
Crab-filled Enchiladas

These crab enchiladas are delicious and probably more common in Austin, Texas than anywhere else in the world. Microwave ovens are particularly good for heating frozen crab legs.

8 Enchiladas

    8 corn tortillas
  1/2 lb. crab meat or 2 lbs. of crab legs
    1 teaspoon olive oil
  1/2 medium onion, sliced
    2 garlic cloves, chopped
    1 small tomato, chopped
  1/4 teaspoon cayenne
  1/4 cup water or white wine
  1/2 teaspoon oil for the baking dish
    4 ounces grated jack cheese
       Salt and black pepper to taste

Procedures

Heat frozen crab legs in the microwave oven for eight minutes on HIGH in an uncovered dish. Drain the water from the dish and allow the legs to cool before removing the crab meat.

Heat the olive oil. Add onions and garlic and brown both slightly. Add the tomato and mix the ingredients.

Add the crab meat, spices, and water or white wine.

Simmer on low heat for about ten minutes. After ten minutes, drain most of the remaining liquid from the mixture leaving only two or three tablespoons of liquid for moisture.

Using the procedures in "Enchiladas Perfectas," moisten each tortilla, heat it, and fill it with the crab meat mixture.

Place each rolled tortilla in a slightly oiled baking dish with the seam side down to prevent the tortilla from opening. Repeat this procedure for each of the eight tortillas.

Top the enchiladas with jack cheese. Other cheeses can also be used if preferred.

Heat the enchiladas in the oven for only five minutes at 400°.

Remove and serve with red or green enchilada sauce or with a simple salsa de tomate y chile.

Microwave oven

Heat two pounds of frozen crab legs on HIGH for eight minutes. Remove the meat from the legs and claws.

Follow the procedures described above using the ingredients listed to make the crab meat filling.

Roll each heated tortilla and assemble in a slightly oiled baking dish. Top with grated cheese.

Heat on HIGH for three minutes before removing and serving.

ENCHILADAS LAS CRUCES

New Mexico-style enchiladas are often served stacked rather than rolled. The sauce is formed using the "New Mexico Red Pepper Sauce" recipe as the basis.

12 Enchiladas

Sauce

>   8 large New Mexico dried red peppers
>   1 medium onion, chopped
>   1 garlic clove, chopped
>   1 cup of water; in addition to water used for simmering peppers
>   2 tablespoons flour
> 1/2 cup of water for dissolving flour
>   Salt and black pepper to taste

Enchiladas

> 12 corn tortillas
> 1/2 teaspoon olive or vegetable oil for the baking dish
>   1 medium onion, sliced
>   1 medium tomato, chopped
>   4 ounces grated cheddar cheese

Procedures

To make the sauce, cover the peppers with water, add half the chopped medium onion, a chopped garlic clove, and simmer on low heat for twenty-five minutes.

After twenty-five minutes, drain the water, discard the onion and garlic, and set the peppers aside to cool.

When the peppers have cooled enough to handle safely, remove the stems and seeds from the peppers.

Place the peppers, one cup of water, and the remaining half onion into the blender or food processor. Blend thoroughly until the peppers and onion have been completely liquefied.

Pour the sauce through a strainer to remove particles of pepper and seeds.

Dissolve two tablespoons of flour in 1/2 cup of water. When the flour has completely dissolved in the water, add the water with flour to the pepper sauce. Simmer on low heat for at least thirty minutes. Stir occasionally while the sauce is simmering. Season with black pepper and salt to suit your tastes.

Coat a large baking dish with 1/2 teaspoon of oil.

Heat four corn tortillas on a very hot comal. Place the tortillas side by side in the baking dish. Top the tortillas with a third of the grated cheese. Add onion and a few slices of fresh tomato to top the tortillas. Place another heated tortilla on top of each of the first tortillas in the dish and repeat the layering process. Add a third layer and top with the remaining onion and cheese.

Heat the enchiladas in a 400° oven for six to eight minutes or until the cheese is quite melted.

Remove the enchiladas from the oven and cover each stack of enchiladas with sauce before serving.

Microwave oven

Stack the corn tortillas in a dish suitable for the microwave oven using the procedures described above.

Microwave six minutes on HIGH, uncovered.

Serve steaming hot with red pepper sauce.

Serving Suggestions

Use the filling for chicken enchiladas or the picadillo recipe for an added chicken or beef variety.

Seafood Specialties

Lake Travis Ceviche. Marinated fish with onions, cilantro, olive oil, olives, tomato, lime juice, and pepper.

Camarones Enojados. Very spicy shrimp, gently steamed in a white wine and lemon juice mixture.

Huachinango a la Veracruzana. Red snapper fillets, baked with tomatoes, and flavored with garlic bits and cilantro.

Camarones Ahijados. Baked or broiled garlic shrimp, flavored with lemon juice and brushed lightly with olive oil.

Pescado al Mojo de Ajo. Garlic fish, baked or broiled.

Camarones Estilo Mexicano. A "Mexican-style" shrimp, with tomatoes, onions, and jalapeño peppers.

Pescado Juárez. Sautéed fish fillets with tomatoes and mild peppers.

Omelet de Marisco. A shrimp omelette.

Mariscos Xalapeños. A rice casserole with bits of shrimp and scallops.

Paella. Shrimp, chicken, pork, and clams, in spicy rice, garnished with early peas.

LAKE TRAVIS CEVICHE

Ceviche is made and served in a variety of different ways in the United States and Mexico. This recipe uses lime and lemon juice, with fresh tomatoes, onions, chopped olives, and a touch of red pepper sauce and serrano added after the marinade is drained. Red snapper, flounder, redfish, and even catfish fillets can be used successfully with this recipe.

4 Cups

1 1/2	lbs. fish fillets of your choice
3	limes for marinade
3	lemons for marinade
2	large tomatoes, chopped
1/2	cup cilantro leaves, chopped
1	medium onion, chopped
1	garlic clove, chopped
1	small serrano pepper, finely chopped
5	or more green olives, chopped
1	tablespoon olive oil
1	tablespoon red pepper sauce (Louisiana red pepper sauce or tabasco sauce)
1/2	lime to use before serving
	Salt and black pepper to taste

Procedures

Cut the fish into 1/2 " or smaller pieces and place in a glass dish. Pour the juice of the lemons and limes over the fish. The juice should be covering most of the fish. Cover the dish and place it in the refrigerator for at least five hours.

Remove the fish from the refrigerator after five hours and drain all of the lemon and lime juice. Completely draining the juices used for marinating results in a fresh tasting ceviche with a subtle citric flavor rather than a pungent flavor.

Chop the tomato, cilantro, onion, garlic clove, serrano pepper, and olives into small pieces and mix with the fish. Add olive oil, red pepper sauce, salt, and black pepper. Squeeze a half lime over the ceviche, stir, and serve.

Serving Suggestions

Ceviche can be left marinating all night long and eaten the next day. Serve French bread, bolillos, lowfat tortilla chips, hot sauce, and wedges of lemon or lime.

CAMARONES ENOJADOS
"Angry" Shrimp

         2 dozen large shrimp, peeled and deveined
         1 small zucchini, julienne sliced
         1 medium onion, thinly sliced
         4 tablespoons fresh lemon juice
1 or 2 jalapeño or serrano peppers, thinly sliced
         2 small tomatoes, sliced or quartered
     1/2 cup white wine or water
     2-4 garlic cloves, minced or chopped
         5 or more drops tabasco or other red hot pepper sauce
             Dash of cayenne pepper
             Salt and black pepper to taste

Procedures

Combine all the ingredients except the shrimp in a skillet or Dutch oven. Bring to a boil. Cover and reduce heat to low and allow these ingredients to simmer for about ten minutes.

After ten minutes, add the shrimp. Simmer for ten more minutes or until the shrimp are cooked. They should be pink when ready to eat.

Microwave oven

Combine all the ingredients except the shrimp in a dish suitable for the microwave oven. Cover.

Microwave eight minutes on HIGH.

Add the shrimp, cover, and microwave eight more minutes on HIGH. Let the dish stand for about two minutes before uncovering and serving.

Serving Suggestions

Place a small amount of rice in a shallow bowl. Spoon the shrimp and portions of all the ingredients over the rice. Serve with lemons or limes.

HUACHINANGO A LA VERACRUZANA

Red Snapper Veracruz Style

4 Servings

2 lbs. red snapper fillets
4 medium tomatoes, quartered
2 jalapeño or serrano peppers, sliced
1 medium onion, thinly sliced
2 garlic cloves, chopped
1/2 tablespoon vegetable or olive oil
1/8 cup water

Procedures

This can be prepared using either the stove top or oven. Either way, keep the cooking to a minimum before checking since fish tends to cook very quickly.

Combine all the ingredients except the fish in a saucepan and simmer the mixture on low heat for about ten minutes until the tomatoes become very soft.

Set the fish in a large baking dish (for the oven) or in a large skillet (for stove top).

Spoon the tomato and liquid mixture over the fish, covering the fish as completely as possible. Top with sliced onion and several slices of lemon before cooking.

Baking

After setting the fish in a large baking dish and spooning the tomato mixture over the fish, bake at 375° oven without covering. Bake for eight minutes or until the fish flakes at the thickest part.

Stove top

Place the fish in a large skillet. Spoon the tomato mixture over the fish, cover, and simmer for ten minutes or until done.

Microwave oven

Add all ingredients except the fish to a baking dish suitable for the microwave oven. Cover.

Microwave for four minutes on HIGH. Let stand for at least two minutes.

Add the fish, cover, and bake on HIGH for four minutes. Let the dish stand for a few minutes before serving.

The fish should flake easily when tested with a fork.

Serving Suggestions

Use a spatula to lift fillets out of the baking dish and on to your plate. Spoon more of the tomato, onion, and spices mixture over the fish before serving. Serve with lemon or lime wedges.

CAMARONES AHIJADOS
Garlic Shrimp

Garlic shrimp, also called "al mojo de ajo" can be prepared by broiling or baking. The garlic cloves can be mashed with the broad side of a knife blade or with a potato masher. This releases quite a bit more of the garlic flavor than simply chopping the cloves. The quantities of shrimp you use for this depend on how many people are eating, whether you are serving this as the main course or just as an appetizer, and how large the shrimp are.

    2 dozen shrimp, medium or large, peeled, cleaned, and
       deveined
    1 tablespoon olive or vegetable oil
    2 tablespoons tarragon flavored vinegar
    3 limes
    8 garlic cloves, mashed
    1 onion, finely chopped

Procedures

Cut the shrimp lengthwise but leave the two halves intact. Combine olive oil, the juice of two limes, and vinegar or white wine. Add the shrimp to this combination.

Marinate the shrimp for thirty minutes.

Broiler

Place the marinated and cut shrimp on a broiler pan with the cut side up. Add half the garlic and onion pieces to the inside of the cut shrimp. Squeeze the juice of the third lime on the shrimp before broiling.

Broil for two minutes or until the garlic and onion bits are browned and the shrimp begin to turn pink. Turn the shrimp over and top with the remaining garlic and onion bits.

Broil for two more minutes before removing.

Serve immediately.

Microwave oven

After marinating the shrimp, add cut shrimp to a baking dish. Place chopped garlic and onion on the cut shrimp. Squeeze a lime over all the shrimp.

Cover and microwave six minutes on HIGH. Shrimp should appear translucent and pink when done.

Conventional oven

Heat oven to 400°. Arrange cut and marinated shrimp in a baking dish, top with chopped garlic and onion, and bake for eight minutes.

Serving Suggestions

Serve plenty of rice, lime wedges, salad, and hot sauce. Frijoles charros topped with freshly snipped cilantro also go well with this dish. Corn tortillas, French bread, or bolillos are recommended.

PESCADO AL MOJO DE AJO
Garlic Fish

Red snapper is commonly used in Mexico for this dish. Other types of reasonably thick (1/2" to 1" thick) fish can also be used successfully. This dish is often prepared on the stove top rather than by broiling or baking. Broiling or baking, however, significantly reduces the oil needed for preparation. Extra care should be taken to avoid overcooking.

Serves 4

- 2 lbs. fish fillets
- 8 garlic cloves, mashed into pieces
- 1 lemon, thinly sliced
- 1/4 cup cilantro, chopped
  Dash of red tabasco pepper sauce or similar sauce
  Juice of 2 limes
  Salt and black pepper to taste

Procedures

Set fish on a platter and cover with lime juice. If baking, sprinkle one side with all the finely chopped or mashed garlic, just a dash of black pepper, red pepper sauce, and salt. Top with thin lemon slices. If you are broiling the fish, use only half the garlic and save the other half to use after turning the fish. Set the fish aside for twenty minutes.

Baking

Heat oven to 400°. Bake for eight minutes and check to see if the fish has begun to flake in the thickest part. If you feel that it is not quite done, bake for two more minutes and remove. It should be done by this time. Serve with bits of fresh cilantro and lemon wedges.

Broiling

This preferred method results in a fillet with a slightly crusty texture and crispy garlic bits. Broil 4" from the flame or heating element for only four minutes. Remove and turn the fish over. Add the remaining garlic and broil for another two minutes. Check to see if it is done. If not, broil for only one more minute before checking it again.

Serving Suggestions

Before baking, top the fish with sliced green onions and a few pimiento bits. Serve a hot sauce on the side with rice and a vegetable such as steamed squash or a salad.

CAMARONES ESTILO MEXICANO

Mexican-Style Shrimp

Serves 4

- 2 dozen medium or large shrimp, peeled, cleaned, and deveined
- 1/2 tablespoon olive oil
- 2 medium tomatoes, sliced
- 1 medium onion, sliced thinly
- 1 garlic clove, chopped
- 2 small jalapeño or serrano peppers, sliced
- 1 cup warm water
- 1/4 teaspoon ground cumin
   Salt and black pepper to taste

Procedures

Sauté tomatoes, onion, garlic, and peppers in the olive oil. After cooking for five minutes, add water and cumin. Simmer for ten more minutes.

Add shrimp, cover, and simmer on low heat for ten minutes or until the shrimp are cooked. The mixture should be soupy and can be made for appetizers or as the main course.

Microwave oven

Combine all ingredients except the shrimp and oil in a baking dish large enough to easily accommodate all the shrimp. Cover and microwave for four minutes on HIGH.

Add the shrimp, cover, and microwave six minutes on HIGH. Let stand for at least two minutes before checking.

Serving Suggestions

Serve bolillos or French bread with the shrimp.

PESCADO JUAREZ

This is named after the city of Juárez, in the state of Chihuahua, México.

Serves 4

2 lbs. fish fillets
1 tablespoon olive oil
2 limes
1/2 teaspoon red pepper sauce such as tabasco sauce
1/4 cup cilantro, chopped
Salt and black pepper to taste

Procedures

Cut each fillet into two or three pieces.

Combine the juice of two limes and the red pepper sauce and moisten each side of the pieces of fish with the mixture.

Season both sides of each piece of fish with a dash of black pepper and salt.

Heat the olive oil in a large skillet. Reduce heat to medium.

Sauté several pieces of fish at a time for three minutes on each side, using a spatula to prevent sticking.

Top with fresh cilantro and serve immediately with lime or lemon wedges, rice, and hot sauce.

OMELET DE MARISCO
Shellfish Omelet

This omelette, also called a "tortilla," was served in Jalapa, Veracruz, with bolillos and hot sauce. The major ingredients besides the eggs were shrimp and a few small pieces of red snapper and sausage. It was cooked in an oven to a point where it browned slightly. This recipe uses shrimp and can be cooked on the stove top, in a conventional oven, or in a microwave oven. If you choose to use the microwave oven, you will have to do without the browned surface. By the time you add the shrimp, it should have already been peeled and boiled for about five or six minutes. The shrimp will only be in the egg mixture for the last part of the cooking time.

Serves 2

- 4 eggs, with yolks and whites separated
- 6 medium shrimp, peeled, cleaned, deveined, and boiled for six minutes. Cut the shrimp into smaller pieces before using.
- 1/2 tablespoon vegetable or olive oil
- 1/4 cup chopped onion
- 1 small jalapeño or serrano pepper, chopped
  A few drops of red chile sauce such as tabasco sauce
  Salt and black pepper to taste

Procedures

Beat the egg whites and the yolks separately. The egg whites should be stiff enough to make small peaks. Pour the beaten yolks over the egg whites and fold the yolks in.

A large pie plate or a standard omelette pan is very useful for this recipe. Use a nonstick pan if you have one. Otherwise, use only 1/2 tablespoon of oil to coat the pan. A large iron skillet is also useful for preparing this dish if you will be using the conventional oven to cook.

Stove top

Pour the egg mixture into the oiled skillet or pan and spread it over the entire bottom of the dish. If you use the stovetop, cook this on low heat until you notice that the egg is starting to set.

Occasionally, run a spatula underneath the mixture to make sure that it doesn't stick.

After the egg sets firmly yet is still moist on the exposed top, add the chopped shrimp, onion, pepper, salt, black pepper, and a few drops of tabasco or red pepper sauce. Fold the mixture in half and cook for another ten minutes on very low heat. Again, occasionally run the spatula underneath it to keep it from sticking. When you note that the mixture has become lightly browned and the eggs are cooked, remove from the stove and serve.

Microwave oven

Coat a microwave oven baking dish with a small amount of oil.

Fold together the yolks and beaten egg whites and pour the mixture into the dish.

Microwave uncovered for three minutes on MEDIUM. Rotate the dish 1/2 turn. Microwave for two more minutes on MEDIUM. Rotate and microwave for one minute on HIGH. By this time, the egg mixture should be firm enough in the center so that it doesn't shake when the dish is moved.

Spoon the cut shrimp into the center of the egg mixture and fold the mixture in half with a spatula. Return the dish to the oven.

Microwave one minute on HIGH. Let the dish stand for two minutes before removing and serving.

Conventional oven

Heat your oven to 375°. When the oven is hot, place the egg mixture in a slightly oiled baking dish and bake for ten minutes. During this time, check it occasionally. It should begin to brown nicely in about ten minutes. Remove the dish after ten minutes and run a spatula underneath to make sure it isn't sticking. When the bottom of the mixture is firm, spoon the shrimp and other ingredients into the middle and fold.

Bake for another ten minutes, occasionally running the spatula underneath to keep it from sticking. Remove when it begins to brown. It should come out in "omelette" form.

Serving Suggestions

If you find that the omelette needs a bit more cooking and isn't quite firm enough after the suggested cooking time, simply put it in the microwave oven for thirty seconds on HIGH or cook it in the conventional oven for another five to ten minutes. Serve with beans, hot sauce, and corn tortillas.

MARISCOS XALAPEÑOS

4 Servings

    1 cup rice
    2 cups water
    6 medium shrimp, peeled, deveined, and cut into 1/2" pieces
    6 scallops, cut into small pieces
    1 garlic clove, chopped
  1/2 teaspoon vegetable oil
    1 small tomato, chopped
    1 small serrano or jalapeño pepper, chopped
  1/4 teaspoon paprika
       Salt and black pepper to taste

Procedures

Heat the oil and sauté the garlic and rice on medium heat for about three minutes or until the rice begins to turn golden brown.

Add the tomato, pepper, black pepper, and paprika. Cook for another minute, stirring often.

Add the water, shrimp, and scallops. Bring the water to a boil, stir once or twice, and cover.

Cook for twenty-five minutes on low heat. After twenty-five minutes, remove from the heat and let stand for ten minutes before serving.

PAELLA

Serves 6

- 2 chicken breasts, skinned, deboned, and each cut into 8-10 small pieces
- 12 medium shrimp, cleaned (shell removed), and deveined
- 12 medium clams, washed and still in their shells
- 1/2 lb. lean pork, cut into small pieces
- 2 teaspoons olive oil
- 5 cups of water
- 2 cups rice
- 2 garlic cloves, chopped
- 1 green onion, chopped
- 1 tablespoon chopped pimientos
  Saffron, a pinch
- 1/2 cup peas, preferably the small variety
  Salt and black pepper to taste

Procedures

Heat two teaspoons of olive oil over medium heat. Add the garlic and onion and cook for two minutes or until the garlic bits begin to brown. Add the chicken and pork, stir, and cook for five minutes over medium heat.

At the end of five minutes, add one cup of water, cover, reduce heat to low, and let the chicken and pork cook gently for the next fifteen minutes. After fifteen minutes, drain the water from the chicken and pork.

In a separate saucepan, heat four cups of water until boiling, add the saffron, and lower heat. Simmer for five minutes.

Place chicken, pork, and uncooked shrimp in a dish large enough to accommodate all the ingredients. The dish must be suitable for the conventional oven or the microwave oven, depending on which method of cooking you choose. A large skillet with a lid is appropriate for stove top cooking.

Add the shrimp, rice, and all other ingredients except the peas and clams.

Add the water with the saffron and stir the ingredients two or three times to distribute the water evenly throughout the entire dish.

Sprinkle the peas over all of the ingredients, top with the clams, and cover.

Stove top

Cook, covered, for forty-five minutes or until all the water has been absorbed. The clams will open during cooking.

Conventional oven

Bake for one hour at 350°.

Serving Suggestions

This can be made with a number of combinations of chicken, fish, mussels, shrimp, pork, bits of sausage, tomatoes, and peppers. Using chicken broth instead of water is yet another option.

Meat and Poultry

Fajitas. Strips of skirt steak, marinated in a spicy red wine vinegar, and grilled over a mesquite flavored fire.

Carne Guisada. Lean beef pieces, simmered in spicy cumin gravy.

Albóndigas con Tomatillo y Chipotle. Baked meatballs, served with a tomatillo-chipotle sauce, fideo, and salad.

Chile con Carne. For use with Tex-Mex Enchiladas or as a Texas chile cookoff entry.

Picadillo. Ground spicy lean beef, simmered with green peppers and potatoes. Excellent for tacos and chile relleno.

Chile Relleno. Mild green peppers, stuffed with spicy lean ground beef and baked.

Calabacitas con Puerco. Zucchini, yellow squash, bits of lean pork, kernels of corn, and carrot bits, simmered in an onion and garlic flavored broth.

Arroz con Pollo. A traditional combination of rice with chicken.

Pollo en Salsa Roja. Chicken in red tomato and ancho pepper sauce.

Pechugas Rellenas. Chicken breasts, filled with onion, mushroom, and cilantro.

Tacos de Pollo Adobado. Tacos made with chicken marinated in tarragon flavored vinegar and spices.

Flautas al Horno. Baked and crispy lowfat chicken flautas.

Pollo en Salsa Chipotle. Pieces of chicken breast simmered in the smoky flavor of a chipotle pepper sauce.

Pollo Rostizado. Basted chicken, cooked slowly on an outdoor grill or in the oven indoors.

FAJITAS

A few years ago, fajitas (pronounced fah-hee-tas) burst upon the scene in Texas and across the country. Served with "pico de gallo" and hot corn tortillas, fajitas are an absolute feast. "Frijoles Charros" usually accompany the grilled strips of marinated beef, and beans cooked and served this way could never taste better. The beans are served as a soup, with a garnish of cilantro. The recipe for beans is included in this book.

Serves 4

- 2 lbs. beef skirt steak
- 4 cups of water
- 2 tablespoons of worcestershire sauce
- 1 teaspoon of tabasco sauce or other Louisiana red sauce
- 2 tablespoons of red wine vinegar with garlic
- 1 small onion, chopped
- 1 garlic clove, chopped
- 1/2 tablespoon black pepper
- 1/2 tablespoon garlic powder
  - Juice of a half lemon or lime.

Procedures

With a very sharp knife, remove the thin white membrane covering one side of the strip of meat. Remove all visible fat. Tenderize the meat with a utensil designed for this purpose or by lightly pounding the meat with the blade of a knife or cleaver. Take care not to cut the meat while doing this.

Prepare the marinade by combining the water, worcestershire sauce, tabasco sauce or other red pepper sauce, lemon or lime juice, onion, red wine vinegar, and garlic.

Sprinkle the meat liberally with black pepper and garlic powder. Place the meat into the marinade. The marinade should just cover the meat.

Cover the dish and marinate the meat in the refrigerator for at least four hours.

After the meat is marinated, it can be broiled in your oven, cooked quickly over a bed of coals or on a gas grill, or smoked slowly on a grill with a cover on it. You can cook large strips of the meat and cut them up after they're cooked, or you can cut them into four-inch-long, thin strips, throw them on the grill, and cook them for forty-five minutes or more. How fajitas are cooked isn't as important as the fact that they have been marinated.

Fajitas are often cooked using a fire built with pieces of wood from the mesquite tree. Alternatives to the full mesquite fire are the commercial mesquite charcoal that can now be purchased or the mesquite blocks soaked in water prior to using.

Using the slower smoking method on an outdoor grill, cook two or three 6" x 12" pieces of meat at one time. Once the meat goes on to the grill, cover the grill, and cook the meat for forty-five minutes. Turn the meat after the first forty-five minutes and cook until done, usually about another forty-five minutes.

If you broil the fajitas in your oven, use a broiler pan set no more than six inches from the heating element. Broil for ten minutes, turn the meat, and broil for another ten minutes or until done to your liking.

Serving Suggestions

After the fajitas are cooked, cut the meat into taco-size strips, about 1/4" inch thick and three or four inches long. You can wrap these in foil, put them back on the grill or in the oven until everything else is ready.

If you like the sound of "sizzling" fajitas, heat a cast-iron skillet on the stove or grill, add the piping-hot fajitas, sprinkle a few drops of water on the skillet with the meat, and you will have sizzling fajitas ready to serve.

After you've cooked fajitas a couple of times, you'll be adding other ingredients to the marinade, cooking a bit longer or not quite as long, covering the grill sometimes, leaving it uncovered at other times, and in general, adding your own tastes to the preparation of this dish. Enjoy the versatility, serve them buffet-style outdoors, with plenty of trimmings of onion, pico de gallo, tortillas, and of course, the beans.

CARNE GUISADA
Simmered Beef Tips

Serves 4

- 2 lbs. top round steak
- 1 large onion, sliced
- 2 garlic cloves, chopped
- 1 jalapeño or serrano pepper, sliced
- 1 tomato, sliced
- 1 teaspoon ground cumin
- 1/2 teaspoon black pepper
- 1 teaspoon chile powder, red pepper flakes, or ground cayenne
- 1 teaspoon olive or vegetable oil
- 1 teaspoon crushed oregano
- 2 cups water
- 1 tablespoon flour
- 1 tablespoon worcestershire sauce

Procedures

Cut the steak into cubes of about 1/4" to 1/2" square. Heat one teaspoon of oil and place half of the onion and garlic into the hot oil. Stir until the garlic and onion begin to brown.

Turn the heat to medium-low and place the meat in the skillet with the garlic and onion. Cook for fifteen minutes, stirring occasionally and watching for accumulations of oil coming out of the meat.

NOTE: If the heat is on too high, the meat will sear and not as much oil will be released. This is a perfect opportunity to use a wok if you have one. As the meat cooks, move the pieces up the sides of the wok allowing the oil and grease to accumulate in the center of the wok.

Spoon out any accumulations of oil as you continue to cook, stirring occasionally.

After twenty minutes of cooking, drain the skillet of all liquids. Rinse the skillet thoroughly with hot water. Replace the meat in a cleaned skillet and add the remaining ingredients except for the water and the worcestershire sauce.

Mix the flour, water, and worcestershire sauce in a separate container. Add the flour, water, and worcestershire sauce mixture to the meat and spice mixture.

Cook on medium heat, covered, for approximately one hour or until the meat crumbles easily and the water has become gravy-like. Stir occasionally. Add additional spices to suit your tastes.

Serving Suggestions

Carne guisada can be served in taco form using corn tortillas. It is also commonly served on a plate with rice, beans, bolillos, and a lettuce and tomato salad. A small bowl of hot sauce should also be available.

ALBONDIGAS CON TOMATILLO Y CHIPOTLE
Meatballs with Tomatillo and Chipotle

12 Meatballs

Albóndigas

1 lb. top round steak, ground
1/4 teaspoon whole cumin seeds
1/2 teaspoon minced mint leaves
1/2 teaspoon rosemary
2 cloves garlic, minced
1 small onion, finely chopped
1 green onion, finely chopped
1 small serrano, finely chopped
2 tablespoons chopped cilantro
1/2 teaspoon oregano
1/4 teaspoon black pepper
1/4 teaspoon cayenne

Tomatillo-Chipotle Sauce

10 tomatillos
1 large red tomato
1 small onion, chopped
2 garlic cloves, chopped
2 chipotle peppers, dried or pickled
1 large jalapeño or serrano pepper, chopped
1 teaspoon ground cumin
2 tablespoons flour
1 cup of water for dissolving flour
2 cups of water; in addition to water used for simmering peppers
Salt and black pepper to taste

Procedures

Albóndigas

Cut the round steak into small pieces prior to grinding it in the food processor. Add the pieces of meat and all the other ingredients listed under "Albóndigas" to the food processor.

NOTE: You may have to grind the meat and ingredients for the meatballs in two portions depending on the size of your food processor. If this is the case, use half the ingredients listed under "Albóndigas" for each portion.

Grind the meat and spices until most of the ingredients have broken down into very small pieces. Remove the meat mixture and repeat for the second half if necessary.

Divide the meat mixture into at least twelve portions. Form each portion into a meatball. The meatballs should not be rolled too tightly since they have a tendency to dry out during the baking process. Cover the meatballs and refrigerate until you are ready to bake them.

Tomatillo-Chipotle Sauce

Remove the covers and stems from the tomatillos and place them in a sauce pan with enough water to cover them. Add the red tomato and the chipotle peppers and simmer on low heat for at least ten minutes.

Drain the water from the tomatillos, tomato, and chipotle peppers. Remove the stems from the chipotles and when they are cool enough to handle, slice them open and remove as many seeds as possible.

Add the tomatillos to a blender or food processor. Add one cup of water. Blend the tomatillos and water into a smooth sauce.

Pour the tomatillo sauce through a strainer to remove most of the tomatillo seeds. Return the strained sauce to the blender or food processor.

Add the tomato, chipotle peppers, chopped onion, garlic, and serrano or jalapeño to the blender or food processor with the tomatillo sauce. Add the cumin and blend until the mixture is very smooth.

Dissolve two tablespoons of flour in a cup of water and add to the sauce in the blender. Blend again for a few seconds.

Add one cup of water to a saucepan and pour the tomatillo-chipotle sauce into the saucepan. Simmer the sauce for thirty minutes on low heat, stirring occasionally.

Baking the Albóndigas

Heat the oven to 375°. Place the meatballs on a broiler pan and bake for twenty minutes.

Remove the broiler pan with the meatballs, brush the brown side of each meatball lightly with plain water, and turn each one over.

Return the meatballs to the oven and bake for another fifteen minutes. Remove the meatballs and gently puncture each one with a fork two or three times. This will allow the meatballs to absorb more of the tomatillo-chipotle sauce when you combine them.

Add the meatballs to the simmering tomatillo-chipotle sauce. Stir them once or twice and simmer for fifteen minutes or until you are ready to eat.

Serving Suggestions

The meatballs should be formed tightly enough to stay together during the baking. Once they have baked, they will remain intact as they simmer in the sauce. Serve with rice, fideo, bolillos, or corn tortillas.

CHILE CON CARNE

4 Servings

1	lb. top round steak, ground, shredded, or cut into small pieces
1	tablespoon chile powder or cayenne
1	tablespoon tabasco or other red sauce
1	tablespoon paprika
1	tablespoon worcestershire sauce
1	tablespoon crushed oregano
1	tablespoon ground cumin
1	tablespoon garlic powder
1	tablespoon black pepper
3	medium tomatoes, chopped
1	medium onion, chopped
1 or 2	medium jalapeño or serrano peppers, chopped
2	garlic cloves, chopped
5	cups water or beef stock (or 3 cups water & 2 cups dark beer)
1	bay leaf

Procedures

Heat a skillet or wok using the medium heat setting. Add the beef to the hot pan. Do not sear the meat. Just let it heat thoroughly and watch for the release of grease from the meat. If you are using a wok, you can begin to spoon out the grease as it gathers in the bottom.

After about ten minutes of cooking and stirring, add one cup of water and simmer the beef for ten more minutes. After ten minutes, drain the water and any accumulated grease from the skillet or wok.

Rinse the pan and return it to the stove. Replace the meat and add all the remaining ingredients including the rest of the water. Simmer on medium heat for about 1 1/2 hours, stirring occasionally. Check the level of the liquid occasionally. The meat and tomatoes should be completely broken down and the mixture should be fairly thick. Flavor the chile with additional cayenne or peppers. Cheese enchiladas topped with this mixture and cheddar cheese result in a genuine Tex-Mex enchilada. It can also be eaten "solo," topped with chopped onion, pickled jalapeños, and a little cheese.

PICADILLO
Ground Beef Hash

4 Servings

  1 lb. top round steak
  1 small onion, chopped
  2 garlic cloves, chopped
  2 small tomatoes, chopped or slightly blended
  1 cup of water
1/2 teaspoon powdered cumin
1/2 teaspoon paprika
     Dash of cayenne pepper
  1 serrano pepper, sliced
1/2 teaspoon crushed oregano
  1 medium bell pepper (mild green pepper), chopped
  1 small potato, peeled and diced
     Salt and black pepper to taste

Procedures

In a food processor or with a knife, cut the meat into very small pieces before cooking. Heat a large pan (a wok is excellent for this) and add half the onion, half the garlic, and the meat. Cook on medium heat for fifteen minutes, stirring often to minimize sticking, spooning out liquid and oil as it forms in the bottom of the pan.

Place the tomatoes into a food processor or blender and add water, cumin, paprika, cayenne, salt, black pepper, serrano, oregano, and the remainder of the onion and garlic. Blend into a sauce.

After the meat has cooked for fifteen minutes, drain the liquid and fat from the meat using a colander. Return the pan and meat to the stove.

Add the tomato mixture, chopped bell pepper, and the potato to the meat. Cover and let the mixture simmer on medium-low heat for thirty minutes or until you are ready to serve it.

Serving Suggestions

This is a delicious mixture that can be served with beans, rice, and tortillas as a simple Tex-Mex meal. Or, you can heat a corn tortilla, add a bit of picadillo to make a taco, and top it with some hot sauce and a very small amount of cheese. You can also use the picadillo to make a "chile relleno" using the next recipe.

CHILE RELLENO
Stuffed Pepper

Chile relleno can be made with picadillo and large peppers such as the poblano, the Anaheim, or the bell pepper.

4 Peppers

- 2   cups of picadillo mixture
- 4   medium bell, large Anaheim or green poblano peppers
- 1   ounce grated cheese
- 1/2 medium onion, sliced
- 1/4 teaspoon olive or vegetable oil

Procedures

Simmer the whole peppers in water for fifteen minutes. The peppers should still be firm when removed from the water. Set the peppers aside to cool until they can be handled safely.

The picadillo that you will use should be warm and drained of any excess liquid.

If you are using bell peppers or poblanos, cut off only the top of the pepper (where the stem is) and remove the seeds from the inside, leaving the pepper whole. With large Anaheim peppers, you may need to remove the stem and slice the pepper lengthwise about a third of the length of the pepper. This will make it easier to remove most of the seeds and allow enough room to fill the pepper.

Fill the peppers with picadillo.

Lightly oil the bottom of a baking dish and set the peppers in the dish. If you are using Anaheim or California green peppers, set them in the dish with sides touching and top with grated cheese and onion rings. Poblanos and bell peppers can also be placed on their sides and covered with the cheese and onion.

Bake in a 375° oven for twenty minutes. Check to see if the peppers have softened to your liking. Cook for another five minutes if necessary.

Microwave oven

Place the peppers in a baking dish suitable for the microwave oven. Top with cheese and onion and cover. Bake on HIGH for eight minutes. Keep the peppers covered for at least two more minutes before serving.

Serving Suggestions

Although this chile relleno recipe uses the picadillo mixture, you can use a variety of fillings such as the filling for chicken enchiladas, chile con carne, or pieces of shrimp or crab. A vegetarian version can be made by using rice or the filling for "Pechugas Rellenas."

CALABACITAS CON PUERCO
Squash with Pork

4 Servings

1   lb. lean pork
1   cup of water
1   large tomato, chopped
1   medium onion, sliced or chopped
1   large bell pepper or mild green pepper, sliced
2   medium carrots, sliced or chopped
1   cup whole corn kernels
1   jalapeño or serrano pepper, sliced
    Dash of cayenne
1   teaspoon ground cumin
1/2 teaspoon paprika
2   yellow squash, sliced
2   zucchinis, sliced
    Salt and black pepper to taste

Procedures

Remove all visible fat from the pork and cut the pork into small pieces. Heat a pan and allow the meat to cook for ten minutes on medium heat, stirring constantly to prevent sticking. Remove excess liquid as it forms in the pan and continue to stir until the pork begins to brown.

Remove the pan from the heat, drain the meat of all liquids, and rinse the pan with water before replacing the meat and returning the pan to the heat.

Add water, tomato, onion, bell pepper, carrots, corn, jalapeño or serrano pepper, cayenne, cumin, black pepper, and paprika.

Cover and let the mixture simmer for twenty minutes on medium-low heat.

After twenty minutes, add the squash, cover, and let the entire mixture simmer for another thirty minutes before serving.

Serving Suggestions

You can make the liquid in this dish slightly thicker by dissolving a tablespoon or two of flour in 1/4 cup of water and adding to the mixture. Also, chicken breast makes an excellent alternative to pork. Serve with hot sauce for additional spiciness.

ARROZ CON POLLO
Chicken with Rice

4 Servings

1 lb. chicken breast with skin and bone removed
1 cup of water for cooking chicken
1 teaspoon olive or vegetable oil
1 large onion, sliced
1 garlic clove, chopped
1 cup rice
1/2 teaspoon cumin
1/2 teaspoon black pepper
2 small tomatoes, chopped
1/2 cup tomato sauce
1 jalapeño or serrano pepper, chopped
1 1/2 cup chicken broth or warm water
1 bay leaf

Procedures

Cut the chicken into several pieces. Add the pieces of chicken to a hot pan with one cup of water. Cook on medium heat for ten minutes, stirring the chicken several times.

After ten minutes, drain all the liquid from the pan and set the chicken aside.

In a separate skillet, heat one teaspoon of olive or vegetable oil. Place the onion, garlic, and rice in the skillet and cook until the rice begins to brown. Add the cumin, black pepper, chopped tomatoes, and tomato sauce and simmer the rice mixture for five minutes, stirring occasionally.

Add the drained chicken pieces to the top of the rice, add the water or broth, jalapeño or serrano peppers, and bay leaf. Cover and simmer for thirty minutes.

Remove from the heat for at least ten minutes before serving.

Microwave oven

Combine rice and all other ingredients except the chicken and oil in a casserole dish suitable for this recipe (at least 2-quart size).

Microwave, uncovered, for five minutes on HIGH.

Place chicken on top of the rice mixture and cover.

Microwave twenty minutes on HIGH. After twenty minutes, let the dish stand for about two minutes before opening to check. If the water has not completely been absorbed by the rice, cover the dish again and cook for about five minutes longer.

Let the dish stand for at least five minutes after cooking ends.

POLLO EN SALSA ROJA
Chicken in Red Sauce

2 Servings

- 2 large chicken breasts with skin and bone removed
- 2 large ancho peppers
- 1 cup of water; in addition to water used for simmering ancho peppers
- 1 teaspoon olive oil
- 1/4 teaspoon ground cumin
- 1/2 teaspoon paprika
- 1/4 teaspoon cayenne
- 1 garlic clove, chopped
- 1/2 medium onion, sliced
- 2 medium tomatoes, quartered
- 1 tablespoon flour
- 1/2 cup water or chicken broth for dissolving the flour
  Salt and black pepper to taste

Procedures

Cut the chicken into six or eight smaller pieces.

Heat the oil in a skillet on medium heat and add the chicken pieces. Cook the chicken for ten minutes using a medium setting on the stove and stir the chicken pieces occasionally.

After ten minutes reduce the heat to low. Spoon out any excess liquids from the pan (rinse the pan if necessary).

Simmer the ancho peppers in water for twenty minutes. Drain the water and set the peppers aside to cool. When the peppers have cooled, remove the stems and seeds.

Add the ancho peppers and one cup of water to a blender or food processor and blend until smooth. Pour the mixture through a strainer to remove remaining seeds and bits of pepper.

Use 1/2 cup of water or broth to dissolve a tablespoon of flour completely. Add cumin, paprika, cayenne, black pepper, garlic, onion, and tomatoes to the water and flour mixture. Mix these ingredients with the chicken. Add the ancho pepper sauce, stir several times, and cover.

Simmer on low heat for thirty minutes. You may have to add a tablespoon or two of water to reach a sauce of medium consistency.

Serving Suggestions

Serranos or other hot peppers can be added for an extra spicy dish. If you cut your chicken into very small pieces, this also makes an excellent filling for tacos, enchiladas, and flautas. See the "Chicken Flautas" recipe for instructions.

PECHUGAS RELLENAS
Stuffed Chicken Breasts

4 Servings

    4 large chicken breasts with skin and bone removed
    1 medium onion, finely chopped
    2 garlic cloves, chopped or minced
  1/2 tablespoon olive oil
    2 cups fresh mushrooms, chopped
    1 cup croutons or dried bread cubes
  1/4 cup white wine or warm water
    2 tablespoons fresh chopped cilantro
       Dash of salt and black pepper

Procedures

Very lightly pound the chicken breasts to flatten them without making them too thin to hold the filling.

Sauté the onions, garlic, and mushrooms in the olive oil. Add croutons or dried bread cubes and add a bit of warm water or white wine to moisten the mixture. Add a dash of black pepper, salt, and the chopped cilantro.

Place three or four teaspoons of the mixture in the center of each of the chicken breasts. Roll the breast as tightly as possible without tearing the meat. Repeat with each breast.

Place the filled breasts with seam sides down on a broiler pan.

Heat the oven to 375°. Bake the chicken for thirty minutes, remove, and serve.

Microwave oven

Place the filled chicken breasts into a baking dish suitable for the microwave oven.

Cover and microwave for fifteen minutes on HIGH.

After ten minutes, microwave five minutes on MEDIUM.

Serving Suggestions

Instead of placing the filled breast with the seam side down, you can tie the breast closed with a piece of string before baking. This is particularly appropriate if you feel that you might have some left over. Use any of the red or green sauces included in this book or you can create a sauce of your own. A dab of lowfat sour cream also makes a tasty topping.

TACOS DE POLLO ADOBADO
Marinated Chicken Tacos

8 Tacos

Marinade

- 1/4 cup tarragon or other flavored vinegar
- 1/4 cup water
- Juice from 1 lime
- 1/2 teaspoon finely crushed oregano
- 1/2 teaspoon ground paprika
- 1/4 teaspoon black pepper
- 1 bay leaf

Tacos

- 2 large chicken breasts with skin and bone removed
- 8 corn tortillas
- 1 teaspoon olive oil
- 2 garlic cloves, chopped
- 1 small onion, chopped
- 1 large tomato, chopped
- 1 small serrano or jalapeño pepper, chopped
- 1/4 cup of water
- 1/2 teaspoon ground cumin
- Salt and black pepper to taste

Procedures

Prepare the marinade for the chicken using the vinegar, 1/4 cup water, lime juice, oregano, paprika, black pepper, and bay leaf. Marinate the whole chicken breasts in a covered dish for at least two hours in the refrigerator.

After two hours, drain the marinade and cut the chicken into 1/2"
pieces.

Heat the olive oil and sauté half of the chopped garlic and onion
for five minutes. Add the chicken and cook for fifteen minutes
on medium heat.

After cooking the chicken for fifteen minutes, drain any
accumulated juices, return the pan to the heat, and replace the
chicken.

Add chopped tomato, the remaining garlic and onion, the
serrano or jalapeño, and 1/4 cup water. Add cumin, a dash of
black pepper and salt, and simmer for twenty more minutes.
Flavor with additional peppers and sauces as desired and serve
in hot corn tortillas.

Serving Suggestions

This is just one of many fillings you can create for corn tortilla
tacos. It can also be used as a main meal served with rice, beans,
salad, and soup.

FLAUTAS AL HORNO

The chicken for flautas can be prepared using the recipes for "Preparing a Chicken Enchilada Filling," "Tacos de Pollo Adobado," or "Pollo en Salsa Roja." Although flautas are traditionally made by frying corn tortillas, crispy rolled flautas can be cooked successfully in your oven using the following procedures.

12 Flautas

2	large chicken breasts with skin and bone removed
12	corn tortillas
1	teaspoon olive oil
1/4	teaspoon ground cumin
1/2	teaspoon paprika
1/4	teaspoon cayenne
1	garlic clove, chopped
1/2	medium onion, sliced
2	medium tomatoes, quartered
1/4	cup water or chicken broth
12	toothpicks
	Salt and black pepper to taste

Procedures

Cut each chicken breast into small pieces of about 1/2" or smaller.

Heat the oil in a pan and add the chicken pieces. Cook for ten minutes using a medium setting on the stove and stir the chicken pieces occasionally.

After ten minutes, drain all liquids from the pan.

Add the cumin, paprika, cayenne, black pepper, garlic, onion, and tomatoes. Mix these ingredients with the chicken.

Add the water or chicken broth, stir several times, and cover.

Simmer on low heat for thirty minutes, stirring occasionally. When cooked, the chicken should be broken up into many small pieces.

When the chicken has cooked, remove from heat and again drain all the excess liquid from the pan. Allow the chicken mixture to cool for several minutes while you heat up the griddle or comal to heat tortillas.

Slightly moisten both sides of a corn tortilla with water. Heat one side of the tortilla for five seconds on a very hot comal. Turn the tortilla over and heat the other side for another five seconds. The tortilla should be flexible enough to roll easily.

Place a small amount of chicken mixture into the heated tortilla. Use caution with the hot mixture and heated tortilla and roll the tortilla around the chicken mixture. Close with a toothpick.

Place the tortilla on a broiler pan.

Repeat the process with each tortilla. Rolling the tortilla without tearing it will take a bit of practice and can be more easily accomplished by putting very little chicken into the tortilla and rolling a thin flauta.

After filling and closing each tortilla, place them in an oven heated to 375°. Bake for ten minutes and check for crispness.

Remove the flautas when they begin to brown. Remove the toothpicks and serve immediately.

Serving Suggestions

Prepare a thick tomatillo or tomato hot sauce to serve with the flautas. Lowfat sour cream can also be used as a topping. Flautas are not limited to chicken and can be made with a number of other fillings such as beef, pork, and small amounts of cheese.

POLLO EN SALSA CHIPOTLE

4 Servings

2 large chicken breasts with skin and bone removed
4 chipotle peppers
1 cup of water; in addition to water used for simmering the chipotle peppers
2 tablespoons flour
1/2 cup of water for dissolving the flour
1 teaspoon olive oil
1/2 medium onion, chopped
2 garlic cloves, chopped
1/2 teaspoon black pepper
Dash of cumin
1 bay leaf
Salt and black pepper to taste

Procedures

Simmer the chipotle peppers in water for twenty minutes or until they are soft. Discard the water and set the peppers aside to cool. When the peppers have cooled, remove the seeds and stems.

Add the chipotle peppers and one cup of water to the blender and blend until very smooth.

Dissolve the flour in 1/2 cup of water and add to the chipotle and water mixture in the blender. Blend until this mixture is smooth.

Cut each chicken breast into at least four pieces. Brown the onion and garlic in a teaspoon of hot olive oil over medium-high heat. Add the chicken pieces when the onion and garlic begin to brown. Stir occasionally while the chicken is cooking and remove excess liquid from the pan as it accumulates. Cook for ten minutes on medium heat.

Add the mixture made with peppers, water, and flour to the chicken pieces. Add black pepper, cumin, and bay leaf. Stir the chicken a few times, turn the heat to low, and cover.

Simmer the chicken for thirty minutes on low heat, stirring occasionally. If the sauce begins to thicken too much, add one or two tablespoons of water and simmer until you are ready to serve. Remove the bay leaf before serving.

Serving Suggestions

As you experiment with chipotle peppers, you may wish to reduce or increase the number of peppers you use. This dish goes especially well with rice and bolillos and is somewhat reminiscent of mole poblano which, while very delicious, has a high fat content due to the peanuts and oils used to make it.

POLLO ROSTIZADO
Roasted Chicken

The marinade for this recipe is similar to the one used in "Tacos de Pollo Adobado." The chicken can be cooked using the oven, the broiler, or the outdoor grill. If you use an outdoor grill for this recipe, allow the chicken to cook covered with the bone side down for about twenty minutes before opening the hood and basting it on both sides. Continue to baste the chicken every ten minutes until it is done. If your fire is very hot, most of the cooking should be with the bone side down and it should only be turned over to brown the other side a bit. Although cooking times differ with each method, the principle is the same: baste, baste, baste.

4 Servings

   2 whole chickens with skin, neck, and organs removed

Marinade

  1/4 cup tarragon or other flavored vinegar
  1/4 cup water
    2 garlic cloves, mashed
  1/2 teaspoon finely crushed oregano
  1/2 teaspoon ground paprika
  1/4 teaspoon black pepper
    1 bay leaf
       Juice from 1 large lime

Baste

- 1 cup water
- 1/4 teaspoon black pepper
- 1/4 teaspoon tabasco or other red pepper sauce
- 1 teaspoon worcestershire sauce
- 1/2 teaspoon paprika
  Juice from 1 lime

Procedures

Split the chickens lengthwise and remove the skin from each half. Remove all visible fat. Marinate for at least two hours prior to cooking. When you remove the chickens from the marinade, sprinkle them with a dash of paprika and black pepper before cooking. Discard the marinade and mix the liquid and spices for the baste.

Oven

Heat the oven to 375° and place the chicken on a broiler pan with the bone side down. This will allow more fat to drip from the chicken as it cooks.

Bake for twenty minutes before basting for the first time on both sides of the chicken. Turn the chickens over and bake for another twenty minutes. Repeat the basting on both sides of the chicken and turn the chickens again.

Bake for another ten minutes and remove the chicken from the oven. Check to see if it is done. The legs should move easily when the chickens are cooked. You can also make a thin cut in the thickest part of the breast to check.

If you are not quite ready to eat after a total of one hour cooking time, wrap the chicken with aluminum foil, add some of the basting liquid, and keep the chicken in a warm oven until you are ready to serve.

Broiler

Broil the chickens with bone side down on a broiler pan with the heating element no closer than four inches. Broil for ten minutes before removing and basting. Replace with the bone side down and broil for another ten minutes. Remove and baste.

Replace the chickens with the bone side up and broil for ten minutes. Remove and baste. Replace with bone side down for two minutes or until done. Total broiling time will be approximately thirty or thirty-five minutes.

Serving Suggestions

The chicken can actually be kept cooking for extended periods of time if you continue to baste every few minutes. Sprinkle with lime juice prior to serving and serve with frijoles charros and a watercress salad.

A Mexican Food Glossary

Some of the following foods and spices will be of interest to you as you cook and eat Mexican food. Keep in mind that the pronunciation guides are written using English combinations of letters and sounds to simulate the general pronunciation of Spanish words. Accents on the words within parentheses are to indicate emphasis and are not necessarily part of the Spanish spelling. The authors assume no responsibility for puzzled looks or outright laughter on the part of a Mexican waiter.

Peppers

Anaheim. These are also referred to as "California green chilies" and can be found fresh in many supermarkets and in cans in most. These are commonly used for stuffing with cheese, picadillo, or other favorite fillings. They also make a mild green sauce when used in combination with tomatillos.

Ancho (áhn-cho). The ancho is a very dark, almost black dried pepper, used for making tamales, menudo, and other dishes that call for its special type of flavor and color. The ancho is the dried version of the poblano pepper.

Cascabel (cahs-cah-bél). A dried red pepper that should be soaked and simmered prior to its use. Its sauce is a bright red sauce suitable for menudo and red sauce for enchiladas.

Chipotle (chee-póht-leh). The origins of chipotle peppers are "hotly" debated among historians and pepper gourmets. Some say that the chipotle is a jalapeño pepper that has been smoked to a dark brown color. Others contend that the chipotle is a specific type of pepper, dried, and imported into the United States. The flavor is smoky, pungent, and very hot.

Habanero (ah-bah-néh-row). Grown in the Yucatán, the habanero produces a powerfully flavored and very hot sauce. A variety of commercial habanero sauces are available in the United States and the fresh peppers can occasionally be found in grocery stores and specialty markets.

Hatch. This pepper derives its name from Hatch, New Mexico, a primary pepper growing area in the United States. The peppers are used in this book for red New Mexico hot sauce and can be used to make red enchilada sauce.

Jalapeño (hah-lah-pén-yo). The jalapeño and serrano are among several peppers used in many Mexican food recipes in their raw form. In Mexico, the raw peppers are often placed on the table whole or in slices to accompany the main course. Cooked sauces can be made with the peppers by boiling them with tomatoes and onions. Canned or bottled jalapeños are also available in many grocery stores throughout the country.

Jap. These are very small, dried red peppers that can be crushed up and used in casseroles or as part of a sauce. They are very hot.

Piquín (peeh-keen). Also called "pequín," these peppers are grown regionally in South Texas and northern Mexico. They are very small green peppers that turn red while on the bush. Very hot.

Poblano (poh-bláh-noh). Used for stuffing or dried for anchos, the usually mild poblano can surprise you with a nice tangy burn. In Mexico, the whole peppers are often heated on a hot comal or griddle to make the skin blister. The skin is removed and the peppers are fried in oil to make sauces or to use as accompaniments in "rajas," or thin strips.

Serrano (seh-rráh-noh). A smooth-skinned green hot pepper, one of the most widely used peppers in Mexican cooking. It differs from the jalapeño in size (the serrano is smaller), and in color (often, but not always, the serrano is a lighter shade of green).

Rajas. (ráh-hahs). Thin strips, usually of long peppers such as the Anaheim or poblano pepper. Rajas of peppers are served with melted cheese and corn tortillas as an appetizer. Rajas can also refer to thinly sliced strips of onion.

Ristras (reése-trahs). The decorative bundles of long red and green peppers that you can see hanging in the El Paso airport and throughout New Mexico are called ristras. The peppers are "sewn" together with their stems using string, and hung out to dry further. Simply pick the peppers off the ristra as you need them.

Other Foods and Spices

Bolillo (boh-leé-yo). A bread roll, with a crust similar to French bread. Forms the basis of molletes recipe.

Camarón (cah-mah-róhn). Shrimp and all its versatility are featured in many Mexican recipes including shrimp cocktail, and broiled, boiled, and baked shrimp.

Cayenne. This imported ground pepper can be used in almost in any dish, in tomato-based beverages, and anywhere you would like to add a bit of zest.

Chalupas (chah-loó-pahs). Whole corn tortillas, baked, and topped with "refried" beans, cheese, chicken, beef, guacamole, or any combination of other ingredients including sliced onions, tomatoes, peppers, and olives (not necessarily all of these ingredients).

Chili and chile. "Chili" is often used to refer to the mixture of beef, tomatoes, onions, and yes, even beans. "Chile" is a pepper such as a jalapeño and is also used to refer to the hot sauce served with tortilla chips and meals.

Chili Powder. This is a commercially prepared mixture of a variety of spices including oregano, finely crushed or powdered dried red peppers (similar to cayenne powder), cumin, garlic powder, and onion powder. It is sometimes used instead of peppers in tamales, menudo, and a host of other Mexican food recipes. When you used chili powder instead of the variety of spices in it, it must be dissolved thoroughly by stirring often.

Cilantro (see-láhn-troh). This is coriander, a leafy herb, also known as Chinese parsley and is best used fresh. Although you can buy it in dried form, the pungent nature of the leaves cannot really be appreciated unless it's fresh. You will usually find cilantro near the parsley and watercress.

Comal (coh-mahl). The comal is a cast-iron griddle made in Mexico specifically for heating tortillas. It has a handle and is also handy for making pancakes. Turn heat on high when heating corn tortillas on a comal. They heat quickly and can be served slightly charred or soft and barely browned.

Comino (coh-meé-noh). Cumin. The seeds of this plant can be purchased whole or in ground form. In addition to being a key spice in many Mexican recipes, cumin is used in many Indian dishes, particularly curry mixtures.

Fajitas (fah-heé-tahs). Also called skirt steak, this cut of meat has just exploded in popularity within the last few years. You will see fajitas on many menus at Mexican restaurants, and fajita giveaways are replacing the hot dogs and sodas given away by car dealership promotions in the southwest United States. The meat is generally marinated for several hours before grilling. Even Chinese restaurants are getting into the fajita craze by announcing the availability of "Chinitas."

Huachinango (wah-chee-náhn-go). Red snapper, a fish that is commonly served in a variety of ways throughout Mexico. Ceviche is often prepared with red snapper as one of the main ingredients.

Jícama (heé-cah-mah). This tuber resembles a large, brown potato, and is very similar in texture to a water chestnut. You can serve slices of jícama raw, for appetizers, or the pieces can be stir-fried in Chinese vegetable dishes.

Mariscos (mah-rées-cohs). A generic name given to the many types of shellfish used in Mexican cooking.

Menudo (meh-noó-tho). Beef tripe is cubed and boiled for several hours until tender. Oregano, salt, and other spices are added along with ground dried peppers (such as those from West Texas and New Mexico) or chili powder. Hominy is added after the menudo has cooked for a number of hours. Many cooks add pigs' feet or hocks and serve it with chopped onions, cilantro, lemon wedges, and tortillas.

Molcajete (mole-cah-héh-teh). A mortar used to grind peppers and spices. The beauty of using the molcajete instead of a blender or food processor is the care and attention that is paid to the actual grinding of the ingredients. You are able to get the consistency of the mixture to exactly where you want it for the particular purpose.

Nopales (noh-páh-lehs). Often referred to as "nopalitos," the tender young shoots of the prickly pear cactus can be sautéed with garlic and onion and served with eggs for breakfast or alongside a meat dish.

Tomatillos (toh-mah-teé-yohs). Although tomatillos are green, they are not green tomatoes. They are ripe tomatoes and are very different from the red tomatoes with which we all are familiar. The most common use for the tomatillos is enchilada sauce (for green chicken or cheese enchiladas) and green hot sauce.

Tortillas (tore-teé-yahs). The "naan" of Mexican cooking, northern Mexican restaurants and southwestern United States cooks use both flour (the white tortillas), and corn (the brown thinner ones) in their meals.

Tostadas (tohs-táh-thahs). Corn tortillas, quartered and usually fried to a crisp. These can also be made by baking, resulting in lowfat tortilla chips that can be used as appetizers with hot chile sauce, and for chalupas and nachos.

Nutritional Index

The nutritional index of recipes presented is based on the following: All recipe totals use reduced-fat cheeses now available in most stores (except when queso blanco is used). Meat recipe totals are calculated using nutritional information for top round beef (lean only). Pork totals are calculated using nutritional information for center cut loin (lean only). All other totals are taken from product labeling commonly available on packaging and from United States Department of Agriculture information.

The number in parentheses on the first line is the number of servings for the entire recipe (prepared as directed). The second line indicates totals for one serving or one item.

Measurements of fat, carbohydrates, and protein are in grams. Measurements of cholesterol are in milligrams.

HORS D'OEUVRES AND ACCOMPANIMENTS

Recipe	Fat	Calories	Carbo.	Protein	Chol.
Lowfat Tortilla Chips (1 tortilla)	1.0	63	13.5	1.5	0
Salsa Picosa de Tomate y Chile (2 cups)	2.4	220	49.4	9.3	0
Salsa de Tomatillo (2 cups)	1.9	152	32.4	7.9	0
New Mexico Red Pepper Sauce (2 cups)	1.0	167	39.8	8.2	0
Pico de Gallo (2 cups)	1.9	222	53.3	9.7	0

Recipe	Fat	Calories	Carbo.	Protein	Chol.
Chipotle Sauce (1/2 cup)	0.6	99	23.6	4.8	0
Basic Nachos (24)	27.0	852	120.9	51.0	20
Frijoles Refritos (2 cups)	1.5	300	55.0	16.0	0
Four Chalupas	11.4	748	143.0	36.6	20
(one)	2.9	187	35.8	9.2	5
Quesadillas	5.1	148	14.5	5.5	15
(one)	1.3	37	3.6	1.4	3.8
Jalapeños Rellenos (12)	2.1	148	17.4	6.8	20
(one)	.2	12	1.5	.6	1.7
Coctél de Camarón	12.3	701	57.3	102.4	692
Molletes (8)	20.6	1332	228.6	70.2	30
(one)	2.6	167	28.6	8.8	3.8
Chilaquiles	16.2	535	85.8	22.8	27
Sopa de Fideo	9.1	692	130.3	22.6	0
Arroz Texano	6.0	354	70.2	9.0	0

SOUPS AND SALADS

Recipe	Fat	Calories	Carbo.	Protein	Chol.
Ensalada de Berro	0	7	1.6	.7	0
Cucumber & Jícama salad (w/o yogurt)	0.7	97	21.2	2.8	0
Red and Green Pepper salad	0.5	115	24.7	3.5	0
Asparagus & Pimiento Salad	1.0	141	33.4	13.2	0
Gazpacho (4)	16.9	290	68.8	14.0	0
(one)	4.2	73	17.0	3.5	0
Tortilla Soup (4)	13.3	714	107.4	34.5	50
(one)	3.3	179	26.9	8.6	12.5
Caldo de Pescado (4)	4.0	350	27.6	51.9	84
(one)	1.0	88	6.9	13.0	21
Crab and Corn Soup (4)	6.6	831	125.9	68.8	98.5
(one)	1.7	208	31.5	17.2	24.6
Caldo de Pollo (4)	37.5	1266	153.3	99.4	188
(one)	9.4	317	38.3	24.9	47
Caldo de Res (4)	41.8	1335	90.1	160.8	380
(one)	10.5	334	22.5	40.2	95

Recipe	Fat	Calories	Carbo.	Protein	Chol.
Low fat Menudo (8)	65.7	2431	261.7	*17.2	*24.6
(one)	8.2	304	32.7	*4.8	*
Frijoles Charros (12 cups)	12.3	3093	584.1	179.4	0
Pozole (4)	61.3	2056	220.9	182.2	471
(one)	15.3	514	55.2	45.6	117.8

AN ENCHILADA VARIETY

Recipe	Fat	Calories	Carbo.	Protein	Chol.
Basic Enchilada Sauce (Red)	6.6	399	81.8	19.1	5
Basic Enchilada Sauce (Green)	5.1	304	59.2	15.6	5
Enchiladas Perfectas—Red (12)	41.2	1569	265.1	72.4	8.5
(one)	3.4	131	22.1	6.0	7.1
Enchiladas Perfectas—Green (12)	39.7	1474	242.5	68.9	8.5
(one)	3.3	123	20.2	5.7	7.1
Enchiladas de Pollo (12)	82.3	2386	258.7	174.2	381
(one)	6.9	199	21.5	14.5	31.8
Enchiladas Verdes de Queso (12)	38.7	1555	260.6	67.5	85
(one)	3.2	130	21.7	5.6	7.1
Tex-Mex Enchiladas (12)	44.8	1349	194.4	76.6	137.5
(one)	3.7	116	16.2	6.4	11.5
Enchiladas de Jaiba (8)	40.2	1427	122.5	134.2	320
(one)	5.0	179	10.2	16.7	40
Enchiladas Las Cruces style (12)	40.4	1421	243.3	64.2	85
(one)	3.4	119	20.3	5.4	7.1

SEAFOOD SPECIALTIES

Recipe	Fat	Calories	Carbo.	Protein	Chol.
Lake Travis Ceviche	28.8	1057	64.4	148.0	252
Camarones Enojados (4)	3.3	412	46.3	32.9	172
(one)	0.8	103	11.6	8.2	43
Huachinango a la Veracruzana (4)	24.8	1376	35.4	30.6	424
(one)	6.2	344	8.9	7.7	106
Camarones Ahijados (4)	17.7	363	19.3	36.7	258
(one)	4.4	91	4.8	9.2	64.5
Pescado al Mojo de Ajo (4)	13.5	998	33.8	189.9	336
(one)	3.4	250	8.5	47.5	84

Recipe	Fat	Calories	Carbo.	Protein	Chol.
Camarones Estilo Mexicano (4)	13.1	395	29.6	42.0	263
(one)	3.3	99	7.4	10.5	65.8
Pescado Juárez (4)	26.4	1064	14.2	197.0	336
(one)	6.6	266	3.5	49.3	84
Omelet de Marisco (2)	28.2	476	16.0	39.0	938
(one)	14.1	238	8.0	19.5	469
Mariscos Xalapeños (4)	4.1	316	56.7	18.2	70
(one)	1.0	79	14.2	4.6	17.5
Paella (6)	54.5	1781	72.2	199.4	633
(one)	9.0	297	12.0	33.2	105.5

MEAT AND POULTRY

Recipe	Fat	Calories	Carbo.	Protein	Chol.
Fajitas	53.2	1405	22.8	198.9	660
Carne Guisada	62	1963	31.6	292.5	760
Albóndigas con Tomatillo-Chipotle Sauce	33.8	1250	86.2	161.4	380
Chile con Carne	31.6	1132	49.5	158.6	380
Picadillo	29.6	1195	72.0	154.2	380
Chile Relleno (4)	29.3	887	61.6	96.7	230
(one)	7.3	222	15.4	24.2	57.5
Calabacitas con Puerco	66.4	1639	92.7	173.5	504
Arroz con Pollo	30.8	1173	71.7	152.2	434
Pollo en Salsa Roja	28.1	976	28.9	146.8	389
Pechugas Rellenas (4)	37.4	1154	56.2	152.6	384
(one)	9.4	289	14.1	38.2	96
Tacos de Pollo Adobado	35.1	1463	138.5	157.5	384
Flautas al Horno (12)	27.8	968	30.4	146.2	387
(one)	2.3	81	2.5	12.2	32.3
Pollo en Salsa Chipotle	26.9	963	35.2	146.9	384
Pollo Rostizado	35.8	948	20.0	134.5	404

*Indicates some data not available.

Index